THE COMING
INFLATION
CRISIS
AND
THE 4 STEP
ACTION PLAN
FOR RETIREES

THE COMING INFLATION CRISIS

AND

THE 4 STEP ACTION PLAN FOR RETIREES

DAN CASEY

BRIDGERIVER PUBLISHING

2014

First Printing: 2014

ISBN 978-1-312-33621-6

Bridgeriver Publishing
74 West Long Lake, St. 203
Bloomfield Hills, MI 48304

www.bridgeriverllc.com

Ordering Information:

Special discounts are available on quantity purchases by corporations, associations, educators, and others. For details, contact the publisher at the above listed address.

U.S. trade bookstores and wholesalers: Please contact Bridgeriver Publishing Tel: (248) 785-3734 or email info@bridgeriverllc.com.

BONUS: Call or email now to subscribe to my monthly print newsletter. It's written just for retirees and I always pack it full of my latest research. Plus travel destinations, insurance tips and much more. Call the office at (248) 785-3734 or email us at newsletter@bridgeriverllc.com and provide your name and address. Let us know you saw this bonus in my book and the first year subscription is FREE.

Dedication

To my lovely wife, Nina, and three beautiful children, Sean, Jade, and Nick who make it all worthwhile. Thank you. Without your support and patience, I would have never achieved my dream.

And to Curt Whipple whose guidance and generosity with his time and experience has been invaluable in moving my business forward.

TABLE OF CONTENTS

PREFACE

We are in unprecedented times and you should be very concerned. The Federal Reserve, an independent entity, acted outside the law in order to 'save' our Economy. As a result, the cost of living could double over the next decade or two. So, my question to you is, "What are you going to do about it?" While you're young, it isn't that big of an issue. Wages tend to keep up with inflation. If you are retired, then you have your savings to rely on. All of my clients remember the 70's when prices of everything skyrocketed. Except for bonds, of course. They were demolished.

When Ben Bernanke was chairman, he advised us that prices weren't going up much, if you don't count food or energy. That's likes the classic remark from the mayor of Washington D.C. when he said, "Our crime rate isn't all that bad if you don't count the murders."

We'll never know if the Federal Reserve did the right thing. Did they save America from certain demise? Were we days away from bankruptcy? We'll never know. However, I do know what *did* occur. I know that families still lost an average 10% of their wealth in the last few months of 2008. I know that most families lost roughly 43% of their retirement portfolios in that same time period. I also know it was the worst period in my practice. I lost sleep. I lost a lot of sleep. And days would go by where I just couldn't shake that turning feeling in my stomach. My clients counted on me to avoid such calamities. And, I'll be honest. I failed many.

But that will never happen again. If we can't learn from the past we will continue to repeat the same mistakes. As an advisor, we are taught the simple adage that we all know,

*"Markets go up and down but in the
long- term they will always go up."*

And this is true. If given enough time I can guarantee that markets will be higher than they are today. But with every investment decision, there is the intellectual side and there is the emotional side.

Intellectually, I can say this all day long, "Relax, Mr. and Mrs. Client, the market always goes up. Just give it time." But if *emotionally,* you were half the wreck I was during the Great Recession, is it worth it? Is it worth it when you are nearing retirement or in retirement to squeak out EVERY ounce of the market gain and in turn suffer EVERY ounce of the losses? I have come to answer that with a resounding, "Heck No!". And my clients tend to agree. And with the Great Recession in my rear view mirror, I can tell you now I have come up with the ultimate retirement investment strategies that provide just what my clients desire:

1. A safe way to get the gains required to outlive your money without taking the unnecessary risk.
2. Provide more than enough liquidity needed.
3. And the best part? The ability to sleep at night. Because as an advisor of those retiring or about to retire, and as the great Will Rogers said, "I am more interested in the return *of* my money rather than the return *on* my money."

So, what will be the cost associated with the Federal Reserve flooding the economy with dollars? Will there be a price to pay? You can count on it. It's simple economics. Increase the money supply substantially and people won't hold on to devaluing dollars (increased supply, decreased demand). And almost without a doubt the result is inflation, maybe even hyperinflation. I received my undergraduate degree in Economics in the early 90s from Oakland University and did extensive research on inflation.

When inflation is occurring, prices continually rise. Banks raise interest rates to offset the cost of the devalued dollar in the future. To illustrate, let's say you are the manufacturer of a widget and you charge $1. For every widget you sell you make a profit of $.50. Next, the Federal Reserve floods the market with dollars and doubles the money supply. As a result, every dollar is now worth half. If you want to still make a 50% profit on every widget, how much do you have to charge for that same widget? That's right, $2. That widget was selling for $1 before, now its $2 – that's inflation.

And hyperinflation is just an extreme case of inflation. All previous hyperinflations that have occurred around the world all had one action in common. During some sort of instability whether it's war, political unrest, massive political change, or a Great Recession, printing money was done on a massive scale. And in all cases, it's continued well past its usefulness for political reasons to gain support.

And who suffers the most from inflation and rising interest rates? The savers, the people who did everything right. The people who are nearing retirement and in retirement and invest in fixed income products who need safety and income. These are my clients.

These are the investors I focus on in my practice. They have the most to lose. They don't have 30 years of working to make up for losses and to ride out the storm. The number one rule is not to have your retirement tied to the fortunes of the Federal Reserve and the ebb and flow of political desires. And don't have your retirement tied to the fortunes of Wall Street!

Most advisors are trained in the classic buy and hold. A properly diversified portfolio will weather the storm. In the long term you'll be better off. I can make a very strong argument that if you miss out on the major downturns, even if you don't capture 100% of the upside, you will end up with much higher returns and you actually just might be able to sleep at night. My strategies are simple but powerful. My clients and I believe that making money is important but protecting it can be just as important.

So, how do you miss out on the major downturns? Well, I can first tell you that the financial advisor you may be working with isn't watching it on a daily basis. I believe that most investors that work with financial advisors are sold a bill of goods. They are led to believe that the advisor builds a portfolio to meet the client's needs and they monitor it constantly. I would wager money that this does not happen. Even if the advisor places your money with mutual funds which has professional management. Most mutual funds are limited by their prospectus to where they can place your money. It usually has to remain a certain percentage of stocks or bonds or a combination. But they aren't allowed to go 100% into cash if they thought the market was headed for a major correction. Even if they could, attempting to time the market doesn't work either. Countless studies have shown that timing the market is futile. Missing out on just a few of the best days of the market can have dramatic effects on your portfolio. The chart below illustrates the difference in ending portfolio amounts if you invested $10,000 on January 1st, 1980 in the market and just let it ride to 12/31/2012. The ending amounts vary from a mere $29,327 to a whopping $332.502!

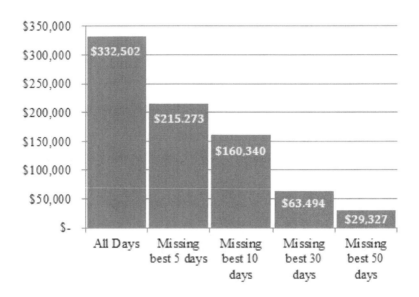

So, how is it done then? How do you miss out on the major downturns while still capturing those strong days without timing the market? I've done extensive research to find the best money managers on the planet. This involves money managers that have a provable track record and the best quantitative analysis strategies. I know, I just said a mouthful. I usually save that type of technical babble when I'm at parties trying to sound smart. Quantitative analysis is simply mathematical and statistical modeling, measurement and research. By measuring certain changes in the market, with data-driven models, changes are made in the portfolios emphasizing long term results and portfolio risk. This analysis isn't always 100% but in my research it does provide a smoother ride.

What is especially important (and most investors miss) are the returns and time needed to recover losses. For example, what return do you need if you suffer a loss of 40% in order to get back to zero? Most investors say if you lose 40% then you need 40% to get back to zero. WRONG. You need a 67% return just to get back to square one! And if you lose 50%, you need 100% return or double your money to get back to zero. If you are nearing or in retirement you do not have the time or the risk tolerance to get a 100% return.

Percentage Loss	Percent Rise To Breakeven
10%	11%
20%	25%
30%	43%
35%	54%
40%	67%
45%	82%
50%	100%

This phenomenon causes investors to take on more loss than they should. When a retiree loses more than they are comfortable with they tend to structure their portfolio with more risk in order to get higher returns and make up for losses quicker. In Vegas, they call it "double or nothing". If the market does go up then they could be just fine. If not, well, instead of lobster for dinner every night in retirement, it could just be beanie weenies. Is this the game you want to play when you are getting close or in retirement? No, let's make sound, smart decisions and invest accordingly.

For the record, I wasn't always focused on the retiring segment of the population. When I was young, I looked at things different. The stock market always goes up. Just look at any long term graph, squint your eyes a little and the line just keeps going up and up! There isn't any other alternative; over the long term the stock market returns are double that of the nearest investment of bonds. So, what are you supposed to do? Take your lumps and put your money in the stock market! To deal with the ups and downs, turn off the TV, don't read the newspaper and don't open your brokerage statements. Sounds simple, right?

As we know, things are a bit more complicated than that. When I started in this business I was only 25 and working as the operations manager at a brokerage firm in West Bloomfield, Michigan. It was mostly a day trading firm focusing on fast traders riding the tech bubble. This was when any company with a dot com after their name was going higher regardless of having profits. The firm was doing fantastic and I was traveling all over the United States and abroad.

But it was at this firm where I learned the brutality of the market. The take no prisoners, you better 'be in it to win it' mentality. The motto there was 'take your emotions out of the trades because emotions make you lose money NOT the market'. Easier said than done when your entire IRA and retirement lifestyle was on the line. I saw it countless times. Investors would come to the brokerage firm and practice trading the market with play money. It was so easy to make money when the money wasn't real or yours. Then they transferred their IRAs and brokerage accounts and started trading. Now emotion was involved. Another saying was 'get in and get out' because you become an 'investor' if you hold the stock overnight. I saw many people lose money. A lot of money.

And no one has to tell my clients the relationship between emotion and money. Many witnessed first-hand the Great Depression. Even our recent ills in the market were nothing compared to the late 1920s and 1930s. During that period unemployment in the United States rose to 25%, and in some countries overseas, to as much as 33%. International trade fell by over 50%. Heavy industry nose-dived, farming tanked as crop prices fell by as much as 60%. Banks failed left and right. And who can forget the news footage of people standing in line for a loaf of bread. Or men who jumped from high rise buildings because one day they were millionaires and the next day broke after the Stock Market Crash of October 29, 1929. And long lines lasting for street blocks of men applying for jobs where only a few were being offered.

I also studied the Great Depression in detail during my undergraduate and while obtaining my Master's Degree. It was a fascinating time in our history. How focused power, egos, and a lack of knowledge plunged the United States and the world into the worst financial crisis ever. Overseas, the central bankers of the 1930s, frozen like deer in headlights did nothing as they were setting the stage of years of economic depression and, eventually, a global war.

So, no one has to tell me or my clients, how emotion is tied to money. And how important it is to preserve what you have. Making money and obtaining the best gains from the market are still important. But getting top gains usually takes a back seat to protecting, to various degrees, the retirement money you've worked a lifetime to save.

If you really would like to know how far back my fascination for money (and how it works) goes then let me briefly take you back to my life as a 12 year old boy growing up in the small town of Imlay City about an hour North of Detroit, Michigan. Farming and crops were abundant and we had two stop lights. And because the population was so small when you dialed someone on the phone, you only needed to dial the last four digits.

You can ask any of my family members how saving money while working was important to me. The idea of getting interest on my money while letting the bank 'borrow' it was just about more than I could take – I was in love. I was a saver. I bought my family our first VCR. The big decision was either Beta or VHS. I chose VHS because the video store had a wider selection of VHS and wasn't convinced Beta was the upcoming trend. It turned out I was right. I believe at the core of my decision was purely because my Dad was pushing for Beta and of course, I wanted to do the opposite.

I bought mostly all my new school clothes and I also bought my first car. However, it was actually a van. And it was clear, although I have no direct knowledge at the time, that I was attempting to see how much garbage you could fit in the back of an orange, rusty, Ford Van with a Windsor 350.

The first job I remember was answering multiple phone lines for various businesses and taking messages. I was 11 and had no business answering phones. But who was I to turn down an opportunity to make $1.50 an hour? While sitting in the small two office, dingy office building I noticed the parking lot of a neighboring business was filthy. So, I offered to sweep it once a week for $10. One day, while my friend was visiting me as I swept, the next business over noticed my fine sweeping skills and wanted their parking lot swept also. However the job was offered to both my friend and I. And even though I wasn't very happy about sharing my earnings, I must admit, I did enjoy the company.

When I would walk home from my day of sweeping I would notice a few homes for sale and how their yards were not kept up well. I remember thinking the houses might sell faster if the lawns were cut. I immediately called the Real Estate Agents to offer my lawn cutting services. They agreed instantly and no contact between them and I ever occurred again. Checks for $10 started arriving to my house on a weekly basis for each house I was cutting – no questions asked. I believe this is when my love of reoccurring income began. Not to mention the love of the wonders that can come in your mailbox on a daily basis (except for Sunday and possibly, soon, not even Saturday...☹).

To this day I still eagerly walk to the mailbox with the 12 year old boy somewhere in the back of my mind. I'll never forget that great feeling of being paid for a hard day's work.

After High School, I went to Oakland University in Auburn Hills, Michigan and received by undergraduate degree in Economics. Afterwards, I received a Master's Degree in Finance from Walsh College in Troy, Michigan. With that love of reoccurring income still present I bought my first home when I was 28 and then another by age 30 and continued to buy about a home a year. The purpose was to fix it up and rent it out. I even ventured into the Great White North and bought a home in Canada on Lake Huron.

I met my beautiful wife, Nina, a Family Practice Physician during her residency in 1999. We built our first home which is where we brought home our three children, Sean, Jade, and Nicholas. As I write this they are 10, 8, and 6 respectively. They are the love of my life and every day they remind me of what's important. I try my best to 'say as I do' and 'do as I say' because I know that even though they don't hear everything I say, my actions and how I treat other people is also just as important.

Soon after March of 2000, the day trading firm I was working for wasn't doing that well. The tech bubble had burst. At some point investors all agreed as if on one grand conference call that the rising stock prices were based on speculation and not fundamentals. The stock market plunged and many companies went bankrupt. Some went away never to be seen again. But some companies like Amazon went from a stock price of 107 down to 7. But, after a decade later, exceeds 400 and will soon have drones delivering my packages.

I was laid off soon after and was left to determine the next step. It didn't take me long to figure out that a Financial Advisor was my best move. I had already received my series 7, 63, 55 and 24 which were the necessary licenses to buy and sell stocks and mutual funds for clients, manage employees and to be a Principal of the Firm. The intense studying and difficulty of those tests stick with me to today. I couldn't let my licenses lapse and I couldn't ignore my love of money and investing and helping individuals and businesses. So, it was an easy decision.

I have to admit the beginning years were a struggle. Nina had since graduated and was working full time. And once we started a family, the hours in the day start to become shorter and shorter as you do your best to divide your time between work and Family. My company, whose name started out different and has since taken on many forms, is now Bridgeriver Advisors. Growth was slow in the beginning but with persistence and the belief there was no other option, I continued. My firm is now in Bloomfield Hills, Michigan where I can offer a boutique service to retirees with attorneys offering Estate Planning, Business Law, Tax Planning and residential and commercial real estate needs.

When Nina graduated from residency she started working for a husband and wife team that taught her a lot. But it was clear that she needed to be her own boss. To her, practicing medicine is very personal and she needed to care for her patients in the best way she knew how. So, we did some research and found a retiring doctor with a busy practice in the small town of Romeo, Michigan. We purchased it in 2005 and she has since doubled the patient base. We have entrenched ourselves once again in the people and the love of a small town.

CHAPTER 1 - THE FEDERAL RESERVE

Over the years of working with clients 55 and older and building portfolio's and strategies to meet their goals it became very clear that the risks of market fluctuation, interest rate and currency risk, among others were important but they weren't the main risks. It was clear that the most impactful forces exerting influence over an investment is inflation.

Since the Federal Reserve has the authority and the responsibility for managing the nation's rate of inflation, those who do not proactively respond to Fed policy decisions can put their hard-earned assets at risk. If you simply sock away cash for retirement you run the very real risk that your all-important buying power will quietly but continuously erode because inflation pushes the cost of goods and services higher.

Knowing how to protect yourself from that potentially catastrophic outcome requires knowledge of how inflation operates and how to mitigate its impact as an investor. First we'll examine some of the ways that inflation works and how the Fed attempts to control it. Then we'll discuss hyperinflation and deflation, which are the worst-case scenarios. Then in the following chapters we'll review some proven solutions that can help an investor guard against the harmful effects of inflation while growing a sustainable retirement account.

If you are in your 40s now and are planning to retire in your 60s, you need to accommodate whatever economic changes may occur over the next 20 years or so. That can be a challenging idea to grasp, of course, because it is so hard to look that far down the road – especially in a rather unpredictable world following one of the worst global economic recessions in history. But it is not that difficult to look back over the past 20 years and make a logical and informed comparison based on historical statistics.

Do you own a home? How much was it worth 20 years ago, around 1995? What would it cost to buy a comparable home today? What about the car you drive, or the gasoline you put in the tank? While today a gallon of gas averages around $3.50 or more – with seasonal spikes or international calamities often taking that price up into the four dollar range or higher – the same gallon of gas only cost

$1.15 in 1995. Now consider health care costs, since that is one area of your budget that you can expect to increase in direct proportion to your age. Can you picture how much assisted living or nursing care is going to cost 10 years from now? What about in 20 years?

There are virtually unlimited examples that can be used to illustrate the impact of inflation on savings and asset value growth or deterioration.

Keeping it simple, say you invested $2,000 in a one year Treasury bill with an interest rate of 10%. A year later you would receive your principal back plus interest of $2,200. The $200 return that you made cannot be considered the actual return because of purchasing power. Rising inflation reduces your purchasing power which, in turn, means a reduction in the actual value of your return. If the inflation rate for that year was 4% then the actual rate of return was 6%, not 10%. In economic terms, the 10% is your nominal rate and the 4% is the real interest rate. By some calculations monetary inflation has reduced the buying power of a dollar by more than 50 cents since 1996.

Within just the past 12 months, according to the USInflationCalculator.com website, inflation in the USA grew more than 1.5%, and got as high as 1.8% in June of 2013.

But the annual core inflation rate that is tracked by the Federal Open Market Committee still remains below the Fed's target rate which is 2%. In April of 2014 Bloomberg News quoted an economist who summed things up by saying, "inflation has stopped falling and is on a gradual uptrend."

That may turn out to be an understatement as we enter a new era of increasing interest rates and inflationary pressure. A number of economists have been pointing out for years that aggressive Fed action to artificially repress interest rates as an emergency response to global economic problems means that the Fed is long overdue for interest rate hikes. Once the Fed feels that the economic recovery is strong enough to handle the pressure of higher interest rates, it will likely start to ratchet those up and keep doing so for the foreseeable future. After all, the prevailing rates of the past several years have been hovering at close to zero, producing consumer borrowing rates that have, in many cases, been the lowest in recorded history.

For years, as a defensive strategy to stave off an economic meltdown, the Fed has also been printing money at alarming rates when lenders experienced a kind of paralysis that froze borrowing across the nation and around the world. They began printing more than three trillion in the various TARP programs and continued printed 85 billion a month. As I write this they have since tapered to printing 35 billion a month but still have no idea when it will end.

The idea was if the United States gets into deep enough financial trouble and cannot pay its bills, then many other economies around the world won't risk investing their money in the US. They will stop buying Treasury instruments, corporate bonds, and will begin charging more to lend money to the United States and to those who do business here.

So to keep the economy afloat during the Great Recession, the Fed pumped more cash into the system to encourage banks to keep lending to consumers and businesses participating in the economy. That can be a clever move in an emergency, because it is sort of like charging your mortgage payment to a credit card as a way to avoid missing your house payments and losing your home to foreclosure. Obviously, that kind of maneuver is not sustainable. Eventually you have to pay off your debts to return to normalcy.

Unlike individual investors, governments can print money, and that may sound like a dream come true. But money is, in simple terms, just another commodity. The more of it you flood into the marketplace, the less it's worth – because of basic principles of supply and demand. As more money is printed and put into circulation by consumers, prices tend to go up, although wages and incomes tend to stay the same. That creates a gap and that disparity between income and the cost of living can wreak havoc on a retirement nest egg.

As currency loses its value, investors typically shift into more tangible assets that cannot simply be printed like paper money. They buy hard assets such as gold, platinum, oil, and other commodities that are in demand around the world. So printing money is not a real solution – it is just a tactic for postponing problems until you can figure a better way out.

When central banks aren't careful, or when they are especially unlucky, the plan can backfire. How bad can it get? For an answer to that we can look at the recent history of the nation of Zimbabwe, where from 2004 to 2009 that country's central bank printed money to pay for a war that they could not actually afford.

Then their financial troubles were compounded by unexpected droughts and restrictions on the amount of food and other goods that could be domestically produced. Prices began to go up until they were so out of control that they were doubling every 24 hours. With an inflation rate of around 100% your money is not worth much for long. That's why people and businesses in Zimbabwe abandoned their own national currency. They started requiring payment in foreign currencies instead. That gives us a stern warning about inflation and it also demonstrates why diversification into other types of investments may be a smart idea for an investor.

The most notorious example of rampant hyperinflation occurred in Germany in the 1920s. The exchange rate in 1921 was approximately one U.S. dollar to 50 German marks. Two years later, attempts to finance an extraordinarily expensive war crippled the German economy and the exchange rate fell to one U.S. dollar for every 4.2 trillion German marks. Inflation was an astounding 14,000%.

In the past, to avoid hyperinflation, the Federal Reserve and U.S. Treasury followed a policy of tying the value of dollars to underlying precious metals like gold and silver. If you are retirement age you probably recall that when you were a child American currency had printed across it the words "silver certificate."

You could literally walk into any bank in the country and trade your dollars or silver certificates for actual silver. That ensured that a paper dollar was equal in value to a silver dollar. But that system ended in 1965. Ever since then, paper money in this country is only valued as a Federal Reserve note, making it essentially an I.O.U from Uncle Sam backed by the full faith of the Government.

Obviously the threat of inflation needs to be taken seriously because otherwise it can even accelerate into hyperinflation, a devastating consequence of ill-advised monetary policy. Many Americans saving for retirement worry about inflation, for good reason. There isn't much comfort in history lessons, either, since two of the most dramatic examples of hyperinflation – in Zimbabwe and Germany – were triggered when nations printed money way beyond when it made sense.

Could that happen here in the United States? A more pragmatic and valuable question for the investor to ask is "How can I protect my portfolio to safeguard against unforeseen economic events if it does?" That's also a great question to ask anyone you plan to hire as a financial advisor.

The good news is the economy is strengthening, but that will require an intelligent and careful response from investors and portfolio managers. There are a number of ways that Federal Reserve decisions in the coming months and years can have a powerful and profound impact on an investment portfolio or retirement account.

As the cost of borrowing increases along with those inevitable higher interest rates, it will be easier to compound your savings by earning a higher rate of interest. The rates paid on products like money market accounts or certificates of deposit, for example, will rise. That will help to at least offset some of the intrinsic low of value caused by ordinary inflation.

On the flip side of that equation, however, higher rates will also make it increasingly more difficult for consumers to pay for bigger ticket items like automobiles, houses, college tuition, and medical care. The cost of housing is already getting dramatically more expensive, and many recent reports describe an alarming rise in the cost of basic commodities such as groceries.

But if you are thinking about retirement you probably already noted that within the past year Social Security payments were adjusted to keep them in line with inflation. The Social Security Administration does that at regular intervals, and it is usually not newsworthy. When it happened recently, though, it made headlines because the payout adjustment was so low compared to the actual rate of inflation. Many retirement planners were shocked to find out that the new rate falls considerably short of the implied goal of keeping pace with inflation. That means that even your Social Security payments are highly vulnerable to a loss of buying power triggered by inflation.

You should also factor in the kind of predictions that were included in a study published by the Natural Resources Defense Council. Those statistics conclude that the share of the United States population age 65 and over will rise from 13 percent in 2010 to 19 percent in 2030 and then to 20 percent in 2040.

While those numbers are not financial, they do represent another type of demographic inflation that translates into financial outcomes. The simple law of supply and demand, for example, tells us that as the senior population grows so will competition for resources – which means that the cost of such things as senior housing and health care will predictably rise due to stronger demand.

You don't have to look years ahead to see the writing on the wall, though, because the AARP reports that by next year the population of citizens 50 and over will represent 45% of the U.S. population.

The point is that while nobody has a crystal ball to see the future, everyone who is thoughtful and does their due diligence can see that inflation plays a major role in the cost of living over time. Since retirement savings is all about covering the cost of living and hopefully paying for extra enhancements to make your lifestyle more rewarding and enjoyable, considerations of inflation are one of the keys to successful investing.

No discussion of the Fed's management of inflation is complete without attention to the phenomenon of deflation. In other words, what would happen if the Fed's attempts to raise rates and boost inflation fail? Let's use an analogy to simplify the concept.

If you inflate a tire to just the right pressure, it makes for safer driving and even saves on your fuel costs. Inflate it too much and the hyperinflation can cause the tire to explode. Then it's worthless.

The third thing that can happen, naturally, is that your car tire can simply run out of air or deflate. The same can happen to your investment portfolio due to economic deflation.

Economic deflation happens when the situation is so dire that there is no incentive for businesses and manufacturers to make and sell products. Since the value of money remains flat, so do profit margins.

Say, for example, that there was no inflation in the price of a cup of coffee at your local diner over the past 50 years. You could buy a cup for just a dime. The problem is, nobody these days can make a living selling a cup of coffee at that price so they would just stop selling it. Apply that same formula to real estate. One of the reasons we buy it is because it represents a chance for equity appreciation. If you thought the house you bought today was not going to go up in value there is certainly less incentive to buy it. The same goes for stocks and other investments, so deflation can bring investment, and investment value appreciation, to a screeching halt.

That is an oversimplification of how deflation works, but it does explain it enough to see how a total lack of healthy, controllable inflation can also be detrimental. That happened to Japan during the Japanese recession of the 1990s. As a result the recession lasted at least a decade.

So, it's about being prepared and diversified in the proper investments. Evidence of that fact is everywhere these days, because millions of Americans who thought they were prepared for retirement lost so much money during the recent recession that their plans were ruined. Many had to go back to work, and the really unlucky ones were left without enough money and without a job or a feasible outlook for a second career.

Many would-be retirees celebrated the spike in home prices between 2004 and 2005, for instance, as their equity soared by as much as 25% or more. Without doing much they enjoyed watching their $200,000 homes jump to values of $250,000. During the first five or six years of the 21st century the value of homes in regions all across the USA doubled and even tripled. Seizing the opportunity many investors poured more money into real estate and increased their liquidity by using home equity loans or "cash out" refinancing to tap into their existing equity and access it as spendable profits.

Then gravity took over and the market crashed, destroying the retirement dreams of millions of people. Within about 18 months home prices had reversed direction and home construction fell by more than 40% while the volume of foreclosures rose by more than 40%. While many retirees blame the housing market and mortgage crisis, that face that many lack proper asset diversification and a lack of balance in their investment portfolios doesn't help.

Sure, even those who were well diversified and balanced still suffered losses. But those were manageable. They did not have to sell their stocks at fire sale prices just to pay the mortgage, for example, and could afford to hold on to their equity portfolios and ride out the storm. Of course, those who were in that position and were able to still contribute to their retirement funds have been nicely rewarded, too, because just five or six years after the global economic meltdown the stock market is once again registering all-time highs. The housing market is making a strong comeback, too, and those who were diversified into gold and other anti-inflationary commodities also saw their assets rise in value.

An experienced financial planner will always value balance, recognizing the need for all sorts of different contingency plans and safeguards. Even Warren Buffett, the most famous and successful stock market investor of all time, acknowledges that most of his money was made by buying stocks when they were out of favor at rock bottom prices and then holding them until they appreciated.

He was only able to do that because he had cash in hand when the opportunity presented itself to buy from distressed stockholders. Similarly, if you were sitting on a buffer of cash when the Great Recession hit you had a golden opportunity to buy stocks and real estate at fire sale prices. That is why even the smartest investors stick to a strict asset allocation plan to ensure sustainable and scalable portfolio diversity.

Historically speaking, investing in the stock market is the best way to offset the impact of inflation and to make your wealth grow faster. If you are thorough in your analysis and take a healthy, balanced approach you can control a great deal of the risk associated with your retirement portfolio by investing wisely and ensuring appropriate balance and diversification. But there is a catch to that and many Baby Boomers succumb to one of the greatest pitfalls of all because they do not fully grasp the nature of the markets.

Just as the Fed is continually implementing policies and procedures that influence the economy and the value of your money, other global market players and events also constantly shift the landscape of the greater economy. Unless you vigilantly and regularly respond to those changes and shifts then your portfolio will lose its precious balance and diversification.

Think about it in terms of a vehicle you are using to get you from Point A (today) to Point B (your planned retirement) and beyond. You may have a brand new car with perfectly aligned wheels, but as you travel those wheels gradually move out of alignment. Neglect them long enough and they will become a hazard. Similarly, assets do not automatically align themselves. You must be proactive about how you manage them.

Your life is not stagnant either, so your financial priorities are also subject to change. The portfolio you established even a few years may be completely outdated by now. Maybe your health changes or you enter retirement and that creates a seismic shift in your income. What if you make more money and that places you in a different income bracket or you downsize your home and that alters your monthly budget? Are you nimble and knowledgeable enough to respond to each of these forces that have the potential to disrupt your retirement plan and your nest egg portfolio?

If that line of questioning makes you uncomfortable or raises more questions about your financial security, don't fret. You are not alone. But you are ahead of the majority of would-be retirees and investors, because at least you are asking the right questions and are seeking answers to keep educating yourself and making sure that your retirement strategy stays relevant and viable.

The truth is, even highly successful investment professionals don't try to do it all on their own. They surround themselves with other experts. You can do the same, even if you are not yet wealthy. Shop around for the most qualified and experienced financial help you can find, and take full advantage of it. We all want our money to work hard for us, even while we are asleep, because that is the fastest way to wealth. But that does not mean that you can literally go to sleep and dream your way to retirement. Someone has to be awake, alert, and adept at keeping that engine running smoothly.

In the next chapters, I'll be discussing the four step action plan that provides the best way to build and maintain your portfolio through the coming inflation crisis. There are clearly more than four ways to prepare for inflation. But I've used my almost two decades in the business to narrow it down to the best ways and narrowed it down even more when considering the retiree's situation. Some are too speculative or expensive. And some, in the commodities arena, just make no sense for retirees at all.

The next chapter is step one and covers Social Security. Probably the most important and least understood. There was a time when the decision to take Social Security was much easier. You either took it as early as possible, at age 62, or you didn't.

Following that is step two and covers smart investing. If you are nearing retirement or currently retiring and your invested in the stock market and don't have a way to protect yourself from the downside then you're making a mistake. Unfortunately most advisors watch their clients' money go up in good times and then watch it go down in bad times and don't do much about it. How would you feel if you woke up tomorrow morning, turn on the news and find out some sort of huge explosion has happened on U.S. soil and the U.S. government isn't certain the cause. Soon after the market opens, it's down by 10%. You don't want to overreact in case this wasn't a terrorist attack. By the end of the day, we find out it was in fact a terrorist attack. The next day the market opens another 10% down and you certainly don't want to sell now and lose 20%. What if this was an isolated incident and this will soon be all over. The next morning the market is down another 10% and falling so fast an unprecedented move is made to halt trading on some of the stocks that are in free fall. So, maybe, you couldn't even get out if you wanted to. Is this hypothetical really so far-fetched? Do you even want to take that risk? How would that make you feel if you lost 30, 40 or even 50% of your portfolio? If the thought makes your stomach turn then you need to take action.

The next chapter is step 3 and that requires getting your hands around a concept you may not be familiar with. This will cover an investment that you actually hold in your possession and are the highest correlated investment to inflation that you can own. You can keep this investment away from prying eyes of the government and everyone else unless you choose they know.

And the final step is to own the next best correlated investment to inflation – real estate. Owning your own home is a start but not enough. There are many different ways to invest in real estate but I'll cover the best way for retirees.

I will also mention, although it sounds self-serving, many of the strategies involve using a financial advisor. Strategies for retirees often involve sophisticated products. Strategies that cannot be purchased by many individual investors. Unfortunately, an investor working on his/her own have very limited, watered down products. And don't take my word for it. Perform a search on the internet about inflation strategies. What you will get are strategies that suggest commodities or money market accounts and Treasury Inflation Protected Securities (TIPS). Commodities are extremely volatile and an investment I rarely suggest for a retiree. And then on the other side of the risk spectrum you have money market accounts and TIPS! I understand that money market rates will increase with inflationary pressures and the very nature of TIPS will do the same. But the dismal rates you receive while you wait until inflation ramps up doesn't work for me or my clients. There are smarter strategies, let's get started.

CHAPTER 2 - SOCIAL SECURITY

Making the right moves can increase lifetime benefits substantially

STEP ONE - In 1935, President Franklin Delano Roosevelt signed the Social Security Act. It was created out of necessity as the United States was coming out of the Great Depression and numerous aging Americans were struggling. Financing would come from workers and employers and be distributed to retirees.

After year of paying into Social Security, it is approaching the time that the largest generation ever will start reaping their benefits. In 1940, the life expectancy of a 65-year-old was almost 14 years;

today it is about 20 years. Having your retirement income last 20 years is no small task. You may have heard of the three legged stool. The saying goes, your retirement income is like a three legged stool. Each leg is represented by your investments, pensions, and Social Security. If you don't have one of these 'legs' then the stool comes crashing down. With pensions disappearing every day, Social Security and your investment planning have become even more important. Recent statistics say 51% of the workforce has no private pension coverage and 34% of the workforce have no savings set aside for retirement. According to the social security website, in 2014, over 59 million Americans will receive almost $863 billion in Social Security benefits.

- Social Security benefits represent about 38% of the income of the elderly.
- Among elderly Social Security beneficiaries, 52% of married couples and 74% of unmarried persons receive 50% or more of their income from Social Security.
- Among elderly Social Security beneficiaries, 22% of married couples and about 47% of unmarried persons rely on Social Security for 90% or more of their income.
- Nine out of ten individuals age 65 and older receive Social Security benefits.

These statistics reinforce how important Social Security is and how important it is to make the right choice. There was once a day when the only decision was to turn in your application or not. Not anymore. And what makes this more difficult for most people is the fact that the Social Security Administration (SSA) is *forbidden* to provide election advice. They can help in providing the highest monthly Social Security benefits. But with some of the advanced strategies that we'll cover in this chapter you can still often receive spousal benefits while your own benefits based on your own work record will continue to grow with DRC's. When it grows to the desired amount (or age 70, whatever comes first) then you 'switch' to your own benefits. Often times, these strategies will lead to higher lifetime benefits than just the monthly benefit that the administration will provide.

With the coming inflation crisis, Social Security is even more critical. If you delay your benefits you receive delayed retirement credits (DRC) of 8% a year. What better way to beat inflation then to have your benefits increases at an impressive 8% a year. I'll get into more detail of how that works later in this chapter.

Let's review the basics of how Social Security works:
1. When you receive a paycheck from your employer, you pay into Social Security
2. 6.2% of your salary is paid by you and 6.2% is paid by your employer
3. 40 credits are needed to be eligible to receive benefits
4. 1 credit for every $1,200 made annually
5. Maximum 4 credits per year

6. 2014 average Social Security benefits is $1,294 per month
7. Maximum benefit for 2014 is $2,642 per month
8. Highest 35 years of earnings are used to determine your Social Security benefit
9. If you work less than 35 years, the missing years are counted as zero.
10. Maximum taxable income is $117,000

The first step in determining your benefit strategy as you approach retirement is finding your Primary Insurance Amount (PIA). This is the amount you'll receive when you reach your full retirement age. In 2011, the SSA stopped sending out paper statements to Americans, saving an estimated 70 million dollars.

However, as I write this, the SSA just announced that they will begin mailing statements again. Starting in September, 2014 the SSA will resume mailings at five-year intervals to workers who have not signed up to view their statements online. They will be sent to workers at ages 25, 30, 35, 40, 45, 50, 55 and 60. The annual statement includes an estimate of monthly benefits at various claiming ages, and for disability claims. It explains how benefits are calculated, and displays the work's history of income subject to Social Security tax. However, it can still be challenging to determine the amount you will receive when you begin taking payments.

You can find this information by either calling the SSA or visiting its website (www.ssa.gov). You may also work with a financial service professional to help you get the answers you need to make an informed decision.

Once you figure out how much your benefits will be, you'll need to figure out when you can begin. The earliest you may begin receiving benefits is 62. However, if you take benefits as early as possible, your benefits will be reduced. At age 62, your benefit will only be 75% of your PIA. Depending on your lifespan, this can drastically reduce the amount of Social Security you receive over your lifetime.

Year of Birth	Full Retirement Age
1937 or earlier	65
1938	65 and 2 months
1939	65 and 4 months
1940	65 and 6 months
1941	65 and 8 months
1942	65 and 10 months
1943-1954	66
1955	66 and 2 months
1956	66 and 4 months
1957	66 and 6 months
1958	66 and 8 months
1959	66 and 10 months
1960 and after	67

Each year you delay receiving your Social Security benefit, your payment will increase. Once you reach your FRA, you can begin receiving your unreduced, full PIA. You can continue to delay receiving benefits until age 70.

Your benefit will increase by the 8% DRC from your FRA until a max at age 70. So, by delaying payments from FRA to age 70, recipients will receive a 32% increase in benefits!

Apply At Age	Benefit will be Percent of PIA	Example if PIA is $1000
62	75%	$750
63	80%	$800
64	86.7%	$867
65	93.3%	$933
66*	100%	$1,000
67	108%	$1,080
68	116%	$1,160
69	124%	$1,240
70	132%	$1,320

One of the most challenging questions is when to start receiving your Social Security benefit. I've detailed when you can and the consequences but as I've alluded to before it is much more complicated than that. Two primary factors may help you make your decision.

First, do you need the money? If you need the income to cover expenses in retirement, your decision is made. If you do not need the money, it might make sense to delay receiving your benefit and let your future payment continue to increase. The second factor is your health and life expectancy. Individuals in poor health may want to begin receiving their benefits earlier rather than later. If you are in good health and have a history of longevity in your family, it may make sense to wait.

There are calculators online to help you determine your available benefit at various ages. By determining your breakeven age and your projected life expectancy, you can make an informed decision about when to apply for your Social Security benefit.

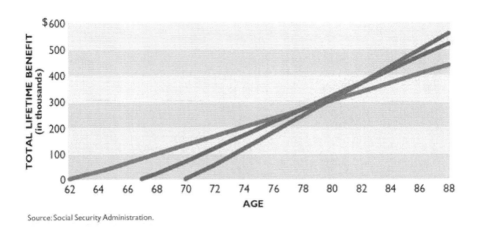

Source: Social Security Administration.

However, the point to remember here is most advisors will only focus on this type of analysis. But this only takes into account your benefits based on your earnings records. This doesn't provide the full benefit package because SSA offers three distinct benefits.

1. Retired Worker Benefit – This is your benefit package based on your earnings record.

2. Spousal benefits – Provides a benefit to your spouse once you start claiming your own benefits.

3. Survivor benefit – Provides a benefit to your spouse after your death.

4. So, it's important that you get the proper analysis. For instance, in my office, we run our Social Security Full Benefits Package Report™ that runs through thousands of different possibilities to produce a report that provides a customized step by step plan in order to maximize your benefits. I've done this enough to see over and over that the difference in benefits can be as high as $300,000 in lifetime benefits. This is calculated from the difference of both spouses filing at their earliest age to both following the steps in the Social Security Full Benefits Package Report™.

I've discussed DRCs however that is not the only way your benefits can increase. Each October, the SSA announces the amount in which monthly benefits will increase. Cost-of-living adjustments (COLA) are applied to individuals who are already receiving benefits and to those who have not begun yet. COLA is based off the Consumer Price Index from the third quarter of one year to the third quarter of the next. There is no guarantee of COLA annually, as we saw in 2010 and 2011 when there were no

COLA raises. This unknown can make it more challenging to plan your retirement income.

If you are a married individual who had little to no earnings throughout your working years, Social Security can be received through spousal benefits. Once your working spouse files for his or her benefit, you can also file and start receiving half of your working spouse's benefit. As the non-working spouse, you may file for benefits before FRA; however, you will receive a reduced spousal benefit.

Two high income-earning spouses can also utilize spousal benefits. One of the spouses can file for benefits, and the other can claim spousal benefits. The one who claims spousal benefits can earn Social Security payments but allow his or her personal benefit to continue rolling up with DRCs until age 70. At that time, one can forfeit spousal benefits and begin taking his or her own Social Security income at the maximum benefit amount.

Most people assume incorrectly that if they have benefits based on their own earnings record they must take those benefits at retirement. But the strategy here is to let your own benefits accrue with DRC's while taking a spousal benefit. This does not reduce either spouse's benefits and is a huge contribution to raising the lifetime benefits.

If you were married for at least 10 years and have not remarried, you can receive spousal benefits based on your ex-spouses work history. Again, you may apply as early as age 62, but your will have a reduced payment. If you have been divorced for over two years, your ex-spouse does not need to apply for benefits in order for you to receive yours. You will need to produce information to verify you were married and for the SSA to locate appropriate records. With that information, they will be able to calculate your benefits. I often am asked how an ex-spouse can attain the necessary information if they do not know where there ex-spouse is. Or maybe they won't cooperate. My best suggestion is to locate old tax paperwork from when you were married. This will contain all the necessary information that the SSA will need.

If you were married for at least 10 years and have not remarried, you may receive survivor benefits. You can apply as early as age 60. If you apply before your FRA, you will receive reduced benefits. If you are over your FRA, your benefit will equal 100% of your deceased spouse's benefit. Your survivor benefit will be 100% of your deceased spouse's actual benefit. If your deceased spouse took benefits early, it will be 100% of the reduced amount received. If benefits were delayed to age 70, it will be 100% of his or her maximum amount. If you were both receiving Social Security at the time of a passing, you will receive either 100% of your spouse's benefit or continue receiving your benefit, whichever is greater. Lastly, if you remarry, your survivor benefit will stop unless you are age 60 or over when you remarry.

According to the AARP, 80% of baby boomers plan on working and because of the recent economy, I'm sure that will be higher. So, let's discuss what happens to your benefits if you plan on working.

Between age 62 and your FRA, you may have some of your Social Security benefit withheld if you earn too much income. If you are receiving your benefit and earning over $15,480 during your Low Threshold years (age 62 to your FRA), your benefit will be reduced. One dollar of your Social Security benefit will be withheld for every $2 you make over the threshold. During your High Threshold year (the year you reach your FRA), there is another threshold income amount that is triggered. In the months leading up to your FRA, your benefit is reduced by $1 for every $3 you earn over $41,400.

The amount of Social Security withheld while you were earning income and receiving benefits will be used to recalculate your PIA; however, the recalculation will usually still work out to be lower than if you would have waited until your FRA to receive benefits. But if you live long enough then it's highly probable that you will recoup the benefits that were withheld. Once your reach your FRA, there is no limit to the amount of income you can earn. You can maximize your earnings without fear of reduced Social Security benefits. So, now that you are receiving the benefits, let's talk about how to keep the most in your pocket and less in the governments. Depending on how much income you earn in retirement, your Social Security benefit may be taxable *and it may not.* To begin, you must calculate your threshold income. First, take your modified adjusted gross income and add half of your combined Social Security benefits plus the following:

1. Pensions
2. Dividends
3. Interest – Even tax-free interest from Municipal Bonds.

Once you have your total, the chart below illustrates how much of your benefits will be taxed.

Social Security
Benefits that

are taxable	Married	Single
Exempt	Income < $32,000	Income <$25,000
50%	Income between $32,000 and $44,000	Income between $25,000 and $34,000
85%	Income >$44,000	Income > $34,000

As you can see, you must add back in interest you receive from Municipal Bonds. Although you may not be paying state or federal taxes (depends on the type of Municipal Bonds purchased) on interest, you must add it back in when figuring your threshold income. So, it's used against you when figuring how much taxes you'll be paying on your benefits. Another notable strategy here is what **isn't** included in adjusted gross income. What's not included is income withdrawn from a ROTH IRA. Because all money withdrawn from a ROTH (unlike a traditional IRA) is tax free. So, it's very important when analyzing your withdraw strategy in retirement how a ROTH IRA can help you adjust your income to stay away from tax thresholds for income and Social Security taxes. For those that have not created a ROTH IRA by contributions and only have traditional IRAs, I know what you're thinking. To create a ROTH IRA of any meaningful size you need to convert your traditional IRA funds. And in order to do this you must pay income taxes (also called the conversion tax) on the amount you convert. This is true; however, what kind of advisor would I be if I didn't have strategies around this also! I'll discuss one strategy here but because I don't want to sway too far away from topic, please refer to the appendix for more on ROTH IRAs.

There are many great qualities regarding ROTH IRAs because of two incredible features. The first is the fact that ALL money usually comes out tax free! There are certain aspects that must happen in order for all the money to be tax free and more important penalty free. That's covered in more detail in the appendix but in general, if you are older than 59 ½ and you've owned any ROTH for at least 5 years then ALL money comes out income tax free and penalty free. Secondly, is the fact that Required Minimum Distributions (RMD) do NOT exist with ROTH IRAs for the owner. The owner NEVER needs to take money out. This makes a ROTH IRA a very important tool in my tool box when positioning my client's money. I can use the fact that my clients aren't required to withdraw money if they don't need to. And, if we do, it's tax free.

After number crunching hundreds and hundreds of conversions of traditional IRAs to ROTHs, it usually always makes sense that the conversion tax is paid from funds outside of the ROTH. However, most are either unable to or want to avoid that at all costs. So, a viable option is to roll the money into a strategy at an insurance company that contains an upfront bonus. Many very good and high quality insurance companies will provide a bonus contribution to your funds if you roll it over into their strategy. Many times the bonus can come very close, if not exceed, the conversion tax you will be paying for converting to a ROTH IRA. Of course, if you compare the best strategy on the market to a strategy that offers a bonus, you'll probably find the bonus strategy isn't as strong. But sometimes, that's OK. It's just matter of a proper amount of number crunching to see if it makes sense. Sometimes, gaining the many benefits of a ROTH without have to pay the conversion tax can be reason enough.

So, creating a ROTH IRA helps in creating tax free income which can reduce or eliminate the taxes you pay on Social Security. Another way to eliminate or defer taxes on your Social Security benefits is to change the type of investments you have that are paying dividends and interest. Let's look at an example of shifting investments to reduce taxable income. When examining your taxable income, determine how much interest you may be paying taxes on that you have no immediate use for and perhaps will probably never touch. This will be the money that could be shifted into another investment. My mantra is to

Never Pay Taxes on Money That You're Not Spending!

And reducing the tax you pay on Social Security benefits is only one of the many great side effects of following this belief. I understand that paying your fair share is important and I would never advise any of my clients on questionable tax avoidance behavior. But let's not pay a dime MORE than our fair share, OK? Listen, the Government will always get their money. If you are withdrawing money from your accounts to live on, the Government have either taxed you on the way or will tax you on withdraws. But if you aren't withdrawing the money then don't pay taxes on it. The idea is to keep the Government out of your pocket for as long as possible!

So, our example is Barbara who is 66, single and retired. She is living off her Social Security and pensions and saving to insure she doesn't outlive her money. Her current income looks like this:

$10,000	Social Security
$18,000	Pension
$20,000	Taxable interest on her portfolio
$48,000	**TOTAL INCOME**

Because Barbara is single her income will cause 85% of her Social Security to be taxable. Add back in the $18,000 pension and $20,000 taxable interest and you have $46,500 of **taxable income**. With this income, she'll be paying $5,536 in taxes which includes $1,775 on her Social Security benefits and $3,761 on her taxable interest. Now, let's examine some strategies that could **eliminate** her Social Security taxes and **defer** the taxes paid on her interest. If we are able to reposition her taxable interest portfolio to something tax deferred look what happens.

Before	After	
$10,000	$10,000	Social Security
$18,000	$18,000	Pension
$20,000	$0	Taxable interest on her portfolio
$5,536	**$801**	**INCOME TAXES PAID**

By repositioning we are able eliminate the taxes she is paying on her Social Security benefits and we deferred the taxes paid on her taxable interest. And her income didn't decrease by a dime. This wasn't about shifting income; this was about shifting taxable money from a taxable investment into a tax deferred investment. And this simple task saves her $4,735 in income taxes!

The main two options to get this done is an IRA (either traditional or ROTH) and an annuity. Some suggest that Municipal Bonds are an option too. However, as mentioned above, many

Municipal Bonds can be income tax free but the interest is still used to calculate your taxes on Social Security. ROTH IRAs in the previous pages were used as a tool because of potential tax free withdraws. Now, we'll discuss them as tools because they are tax deferred also. However, it may be difficult to use this strategy. If the money that you are repositioning into an IRA aren't very large and you are on the cusp of a tier for income and/or social security taxes then contributing to an IRA (whether traditional or ROTH) might work.

The issue arises because of the contribution limits imposed by the IRS. You can rollover unlimited amount from company plans but *contributions* are limited. You or your spouse must have earned income in the amount of the contribution and you are limited to the IRS limit. In 2014, the limit is $6,500 a year if you are age 50 and older and $5,500 if you are younger than 50. That limit is for all IRAs per person combined not per IRA. For instance, you can have four IRAs in your name but you can only contribute $6,500 total for all of them (if you're older than 50). You don't necessarily need earned income if your spouse does and earns enough to cover whatever contribution is planned to be repositioned inside an IRA. Spousal IRA contributions are very misunderstood and many advisors get it wrong. Assume spouse A is currently working and earns $10,000 a year in a part time job. As long as both spouses are younger than 70 ½ then spouse A can make a $10,000 contribution ($5,000 to spouse A's traditional IRA and $5,000 to spouse B's traditional IRA). The age of 70 ½ is used because that's when

RMD's need to happen in traditional IRAs. However, if you are older than 70 ½ and have earned income you can still contribute to a ROTH. There are no age requirements for contributions to a ROTH IRA, only income limitations. If you file a joint return then if one spouse is able to contribute to a ROTH than both spouses can. If one spouse can't then both can't. See the appendix for another ROTH application for children or grandchildren that VERY few people know about.

So IRAs can potentially help when repositioning money to save taxes but annuities are the slam dunk. There are less IRS restrictions on annuities yet they act much like an IRA. You can put huge amounts into annuities with very little limits. Usually the limits are only imposed by the insurance companies themselves, not the IRS. Annuities are tax deferred and also impose penalties if withdrawn before age 59 1/2 however, like IRAs, the income you make inside an annuity is NOT used to calculate threshold income for Social Security benefit taxation.

Annuities as a whole have a bad reputation. And there are good and bad annuities but for the most part the reputation is tainted by bad advisors. They can get away with this because there are many types of annuities and each type has hundreds of variations and inside each variation has alternatives. This adds to the complexity making the decision of what type and product to choose. Unfortunately unscrupulous advisors take advantage. I'll briefly discuss the annuity industry and provide my opinion.

There are three types of annuities:

1. Variable
2. Indexed
3. Fixed

Regardless of the type they do share some similar qualities. For instance, they are all tax deferred and there is an IRS imposed penalty of 10% if you withdraw money before the age of 59 ½. As money grows inside the annuity, you do not pay income taxes on any profit. When withdrawing from an annuity, the first withdraws are usually the earnings first and will be full taxable. However, if you annuitize then each withdraw will be a portion of your original deposit and not taxable and another portion will be earnings and fully taxable. Annuitizing is when you decide to forgo access to your full account value and in turn the insurance company agrees to make predetermined equal payments for the rest of your life (and your spouses if you choose and for a lesser amount). These payments will continue regardless of how long you (and your spouse, if you choose) live. Think of annuitizing like creating your own pension. Say, for example, you invest $100,000 in an immediate annuity and the annual payouts are $8,000. If the IRS considers your life expectancy to be 20 years, divide $100,000 by 20 to determine how much of each payout will be a tax-free return of investment. In this case, $5,000 of each $8,000 payout would be tax-free and $3,000 would be taxed at ordinary income-tax rates.

Annuities, in the most general terms, are the reverse of life insurance. With a life insurance policy you slowly put money in over your lifetime with a much larger multiple lump sum paid out at your death. With annuities, you generally put in a lump sum in the beginning with an agreement that at some point in the future, smaller 'payments' will be made to you over your remaining lifetime (and if chosen, sometimes a spouses lifetime as well). But I've often just used annuities as an accumulation tool also. If I have a younger client who would like to put much more into their retirement than IRA and company plan limits allow, then it can make sense. In that example, it works much like an IRA. It's tax deferred, you have a choice (although limited) of the investments and it's meant for retirement, hence the 10% penalty if withdrawn before age 59 ½. Why annuities work for many people are the incredible and creative strategies insurance companies have created that NO other investment can provide. Certain features are guaranteed income for life, the ability to get a return based on the stock market, and guaranteed return of principal, etc. These all can come at a cost and there are pros and cons to each. Which is why you want an independent advisor that can look at all the products on the market to determine the best match for you.

In some form, annuities have been used since the Roman Empire. Many people would pool their money and the Empire would pay out payments for each person's life. It has even been said that there were instances when the pool of money was maintained until there was only one person left alive to which they would receive the balance. Unfortunately annuities with a lottery win at the end don't exist anymore.

So, the first choice is variable annuities. You have three choices to invest into a variable annuity. If you are a do-it-yourselfer and just want a stripped down basic variable annuity then you usually can't go wrong with one at Vanguard or Fidelity. They also have products you can choose (for added costs) to provide income for life when you decide you need it. With basic variable annuities that don't provide guarantees for income and you get through companies like Fidelity or Vanguard then your money is usually fairly liquid. By that, I mean you have access to most of your money soon after investing with no large penalties to withdraw your money. The penalty to withdraw your money earlier than what the product expects is called the *surrender penalty*. There are two scenarios where variable annuities could impose a surrender penalty. The first is if the product is offering you certain income guarantees. Usually with guarantees there are tradeoffs. In this instance, you are giving up liquidity. However, you know all these details before you invest and usually you have access to at least 10% a year without penalty. But details can differ with each product so buyer beware.

The second scenario is if you purchased the annuity through an advisor that was paid a commission to sell the product. If the insurance company paid an advisor a commission to sell their product they certainly can't allow you to then withdraw your money shortly after. This would not be a profitable venture for the insurance company. Now, just because the produce was sold by a commissioned advisor does not mean the product or the advisor is bad. A reputable advisor should be able to sell a good variable annuity and get paid for it. Most people understand that to receive something of value there should be a fair cost to receive it. In this instance, the 'cost' is not a fee paid by you in any way. The 'cost' is loss of liquidity. It should be said that commissioned advisors are legally held under a different set of criteria. My firm is a Registered Investment Advisory practice held under the Securities Act of 1940. RIAs are required to act as a fiduciary. We must put your interests above our own and declare any conflicts of interest that may arise. The portfolios RIAs construct to meet your goals put your interests above all else. Our only thought when selecting investment products for your portfolio is how those investments are going to help you get to your financial objectives. My clients feel the best part is I don't receive commissions for any investment product I may recommend. The saying goes, *I sit on the same side of the table as my client.*

A broker, or Registered Representative, is required only to recommend investments that are "suitable" for you. In other words, a broker can legally put his own interest above yours when recommending investments "suitable" for the situation.

My problem with variable annuities is not a mystery to my clients. After doing this for close to two decades I have seen variable annuities on a slow downtrend. The more popular variable annuities used usually have very high fees. Even the low cost variable annuities at Vanguard and Fidelity have certain expenses that other types of annuities don't have. This is mostly because the money invested inside the variable annuity is in the stock market. Because of this fact, you now have the added fees of each investment which is usually mutual funds. So, along with the insurance costs of a variable annuity you now have an average of 1-2% of mutual fund costs. As the great John Bogle, founder and former CEO of the Vanguard Funds, once said, "It's not what you *make*, it's what you *keep*". Fees can make a dramatic difference in what you *keep*.

The other type of annuity is an *indexed annuity* or *equity indexed annuity*. The reason this type can usually be better is because your money isn't actually invested in the market. The gains are just tied to the market. This means you save on all those fees of actually being in any investment making this type of annuity very inexpensive. For the basic type of indexed annuity, the investor pays nothing. In general, gains that you receive are a percentage of the gains in a particular index, say the S&P 500. The method the insurance company uses to calculate what percentage you actually get is very technical and complicated. The frustrating aspect is it's virtually impossible to determine what returns you'll get. But with any investment that has returns above a low fixed rate (such as a CD or Money Market) than some variability is expected. But I can tell you that over many years of doing this, the average return will be in the 3-6% range. You'll often hear advisors pushing this product as the next best growth investment for retirees. If you hear that, run, don't walk in the opposite direction. There are two reasons why indexed annuities are slam dunks for many retirees. One, they are principal guaranteed. Meaning, the amount you invest is guaranteed. Just like a CD. However, annuities are guaranteed by an insurance company and CDs are guaranteed by FDIC. But even during the Great Recession, these annuities stood their ground and nobody lost a dime. Secondly, most indexed annuities lock in the gains every year. So, say you invest $100,000 and you end up getting 60% of the return of the S&P 500 that returned 10% that year. You would be credited 6% (60% of 10% is 6%) and your account will be worth $106,000. Your new guaranteed account level is $106,000 and it will never go below that amount regardless of what happens in the stock market. Remember, your money isn't in the stock market; the returns are just tied to the market. You can't say that when you're invested in the stock market. You may have a nice 20% return in the market but you could wake up the next day and those returns (and then some) could be gone! Indexed annuities have come a long way since inception in 1995. For very low fees you can now have income guarantees like variable annuities that many retirees want.

The last type of annuity is a fixed annuity. These are the plain Jane type of annuities and are very similar to CDs in the sense that the rate is fixed for a certain term and there is a penalty for withdrawing early. At the time of this writing, rates are very low so they aren't very attractive. Often times when rates are increasing they can offer rates higher than a CD. Annuities are also tax deferred unlike a CD, unless it's inside an IRA.

So, as you can see, annuities can work very well when shifting money for Social Security benefit taxation. Now let's look at two strategies you can do once you reach full retirement. I'll be writing this as if the husband is reading it and as if he has the higher earnings record. This is so I don't have to continually write he/she and his/her. However, each strategy I'll discuss works both ways regardless of who has the higher earnings record. And married couples aren't the only ones who have all the fun with these strategies. I'll also discuss a strategy for a single person that most don't know.

These strategies will attempt to get you're the highest lifetime benefit. In contrast, the lowest amount you could receive from Social Security (and the worst case scenario) is receiving your benefits at age 62 and not changing your mind for 12 months. Once that happens, your benefits are locked in for the rest of your life and nothing will change. Your only increases will come from cost of living adjustments (COLA). This is in part because you only have 12 months after you begin your benefits to pay them back with the intention of starting them again at some later point in time. Prior to late 2010, you had much more flexibility. Now, you only have 12 months from when you begin. This might be done if you begin benefits at, say 62, and then after 6 months you end up getting the job of your dreams. You can pay back the benefits and it will be as if you never began. This way after you reach your FRA you can begin receiving the DRC's and have your benefits increase by 8% per year. Keep in mind that you have various options of handling the taxes paid on the benefits you received that you are now paying back. If you have to consult a tax professional to handle the necessary changes, it might not make sense if the costs to do so exceed your savings.

The two main strategies are *file and suspend* and *restricted application*. These are often referred to as 'switch strategies' because they often involve the election of a limited benefit initially, and then switching to a larger benefit later. Let's look at file and suspend. This is the simple act of filing for benefits and then immediately suspending them. The main reason for doing so is because your spouse cannot receive benefits until you file for yours. Under this strategy, you did file however you immediately suspended. The key is you must be at or past your FRA. And the amazing part is that your spouse enacted her *spousal benefits* not the benefits based on her earnings record (if she has one). This has nothing to do with the benefits based on your earnings record and her earnings record. BOTH will continue to increase with DRCs. More obvious is the fact that your benefits will increase because you suspended them but maybe less obvious is your spouse's benefits increase too! This is because she is receiving a spousal benefit, NOT her own benefit based on her own earnings record. And her spousal benefit does not decrease your benefits at all. If you are single, you still might want to consider this strategy. Once you file and suspend, your benefits accumulate. This now gives you two options:

1. Take the accumulated benefits as a lump sum at some point after FRA and before age 70 and regular monthly benefits will continue.

2. Start benefits at the higher amount at some point after FRA as you normally would have.

This provides more opportunity. Say, for instance, Betty reached FRA and filed and suspended because she was still employed and didn't need the benefits just yet. Fast forward three years and Betty is diagnosed with an illness that dramatically shortens her expected life span. Because she filed and suspended at her FRA she now has two choices. She can take the lump sum that has been accumulating and take the trip she has always wanted or begin her benefits with DRCs added. The only downside is if you take the lump sum option then you'll receive the lump sum and the monthly benefits that continue will be based on the rate as if you began when you filed and suspended. But this provides options many aren't aware.

Filing a restricted application would be used in order to begin receiving your spousal benefits assuming your spouse is either receiving benefits or filed and suspended. The spousal benefit is half of the benefit your spouse would be (or is) receiving at the time. Even if the spouse has an earnings record of his/her own, it may make sense to receive a lower spouse benefit now in order to allow the main benefit to increase by DRCs. Then once they've reach the maximum possible at age 70, the switch could occur to benefits based on an earnings record. A key point to remember is ensuring the application that is filed is a restricted application if the spouse is at or past FRA. If not, the Social Security Administration might assume an application for the main benefit is requested not the spousal benefit.

After running countless reports producing all the necessary strategies for couples, it seems most couples will want the higher-earning spouse to delay benefits based on his/her record until age 70. The only exception to this is if both are confident they will not live anywhere near age 80.

Another item to note is most strategies are available when FRA is reached however that doesn't always mean that is the best strategy. For example, say John and Wilma are married, both have an earnings record and John is 66 and Wilma is 62. John would like to wait until 70 to receive his benefits based on his earnings record. And he can't receive spousal benefits until Wilma files for her benefits. If Wilma waits until her FRA of 66 then John will be 70 and can no longer begin spousal benefits, he must begin his own. In this particular strategy, it might make sense for Wilma to begin benefits early at age 62 to allow John to begin receiving spousal benefits until he reaches 70. Now, Johns benefits are as high as possible and so possibly will Wilma's upon his death if his benefits exceed hers.

Widows also have options. If you were married for at least 10 years, then you would receive a widow(er) benefit. This can occur as young as 60, or age 50 if you are disabled. And benefits will stop if you remarry before the age of 60. Once you reach 60 (or age 50 if disabled), your survivor benefit may continue. The surviving spouse receives the higher of his or her own benefit, or the benefit of the deceased, which may have been reduced or increased depending on if and when the deceased filed for Social Security benefits.

But there are several issues that can make Widow(er) Benefit strategies difficult to determine whether to claim Widow(er) Benefits early, when to wait, and when to switch to the survivor's own benefit. There are reductions for the widow(er) who claims early and a Widow Limit.

If the deceased filed for Social Security before there FRA then the maximum widow(er) benefit is the larger of the deceased reduced benefits (because the deceased took benefits before there FRA) or 82.5% of the deceased full PIA. I see this misrepresented many times in books and articles I've come across. If the deceased took benefits after their FRA then the widow(er) will get the deceased benefits including DRCs.

However, if the deceased never filed and they died prior to FRA then the widow(er) would get the full PIA of the deceased. If the deceased never filed and they died after their FRA then the the widow(er) benefit would be the deceased's benefit as if they filed for benefits on the date of death which includes DRCs.

To make things even more complicated, widows have two different FRAs, their Retirement FRA and their Widow FRA. For most people getting ready to elect Social Security today, their Retirement FRA is 66. Their Widow FRA is determined by subtracting two years from their date of birth and using that as their birth year in the standard FRA table. There is no advantage to delaying widow(er) benefits past the widow's FRA because DRCs do not accumulate based on the widow's age. As mentioned above, the surviving spouse can begin receiving widow(er) benefits as early as age 60. However, those benefits will be reduced up to a maximum of 28.5% due to claiming early. To determine the monthly reduction amount, take 28.5% divided by the number of months between age 60 and the Widow FRA. Let's look at some examples with Paul, who has a PIA of $2,000, and Linda to illustrate how widow benefits will be affected. If Paul died at 66 and never elected benefits, Linda would be able to claim up to the full $2,000. If Linda were 60 when she claimed, she would receive 71.5% percent of the benefit, or $1,430 per month. If she waited until age 66 to claim, she would receive the full $2,000. If Paul claimed at 62 and was receiving $1,500 (75% of his PIA) per month until his death at age 66, Linda would only be entitled to up to $1,500 under the basic rule outlined above. However, in this case, there is another provision that would impact her benefit amount. It is known as the "Widow Limit," which caps widows' benefits at the higher of the amount of the deceased spouse's benefit, or 82.5% of the deceased spouse's PIA. If Linda elected her widow's benefit at age 60, she would still receive the maximum reduction—down to $1,430 per month—but if she waited to 66, the most she could receive is $1,650, not the entire $2,000. In this case, Linda would not want to delay taking her widow's benefit for any more than 28 months (to age 62 and 4 months) because it would not increase any further due to the Widow's Limit.

If Paul began receiving Social Security at age 70, his benefit would have been $2,640. If he died one month later, Linda would receive up to $2,640, provided she claimed her Aged Widow's benefit at 66, or $1,887 per month if she claimed at age 60.

If you receive widow(er) benefits, you may also switch to your own retirement benefits as early as age 62, assuming the amount will be more than you receive on your deceased spouse's earnings. In many cases, you can begin receiving one benefit at a reduced rate and then switch to the other benefit at the full rate when you reach full retirement age. And you can take a reduced benefit on one record and later switch to a full benefit on the other record. For example, a woman could take a reduced Widow's benefit at 60 and then switch to her own retirement benefit when she reaches full retirement age. Or she could continue to get delayed credits on her own record past full retirement age and switch to her own benefit at age 70.

Another nuance that few know is if the surviving spouse has a natural or legally adopted child under the age of 16 or disabled then benefits can be received regardless if the marriage was 10 years or not. This will last until the child reaches age 16 or is no longer disabled.

A quick note on retroactive filing. The Social Security Administration allows individuals to file for retroactive benefits in some instances. They are:

1. Individuals can backdate the starting month for their own benefits or spousal benefits up to six months. As long as the backdating doesn't take them back to before their FRA.

2. Survivor benefits can backdate their starting month by one month. So a recent widow(er)_doesn't have long before the determination must be made whether to begin receiving survivor's benefits.

3. Children who are eligible for benefits may file six months retroactively.

4. Individuals, whether single or married can file and suspend at FRA and then retroactively reinstate benefits to that date and receive benefits held in suspension.

BONUS: Call now to get your Social Security Full Benefits Package™ for only $99. If you aren't a client, I charge $295 for this comprehensive report that analyzes each strategy and the thousands of different possibilities. It will provide (down to the day) when you should begin your strategy and when you should switch to maximize you (and your spouses) lifetime benefits. It also provides a report about Medicare Insurance and supplements. Every retiree needs this type of report. Call the office at (248) 785-3734 or email us at info@bridgeriverllc.com for more information.

CHAPTER 3 - SMART INVESTING
Reacting, not predicting

STEP TWO - Owning stocks has been a proven way to earn above and beyond inflation. In fact, about 6% over inflation in the long term (if you include dividends). But, in the short term, it can be a different story like during the 1973 Arab oil embargo which sent the CPI skyward. But it helped investors survive inflation in Brazil and Mexico. And it helped domestically in 1971 when the dollar was no longer tied to gold. When discussing the stock market, we must begin with, what many advisors think, is the magic bullet – asset allocation. Unfortunately for many retirees this approach has a serious flaw and can create a troublesome blind spot. But financial planners have been preaching the gospel of asset allocation for so many decades that it is considered an infallible strategy.

Why is asset allocation not enough? That's a great question, and one that more would-be retirees or people already in their retirement years should start asking themselves. What you don't see coming is often times the thing that will cause you the greatest problem, and if you are not vigilantly looking for those hidden hazards your portfolio is vulnerable. Your portfolio should therefore be built on and guided by the fundamental premise or principle of risk allocation – not asset allocation. And proper risk allocation requires tactical management to avoid corrections in the market. As I mentioned in the preface, this isn't timing the market. This isn't predicting, it's reacting. But most advisors react too late so you need a manager who has proven systems to avoid the corrections in the market while still receiving gains. Not all the gains but a significant amount.

Don't get me wrong. I am also a strong believer in a diversified portfolio and intelligent asset allocation. But history and experience proves that asset allocation is only one component of dependable and reliable financial management for retirees. You cannot just put your hard-earned cash into the market – investing in stocks, bonds, mutual funds, and other products – and then passively sit back and expect growth. The stock market can be very dangerous for those nearing or in retirement.

Retirees comprise a very particular demographic with unique financial needs and objectives that do not necessarily reflect the mainstream paradigm. Everyone touts the buy and hold strategy as the best way to grow wealth by citing historic data that shows the robust performance of the stock market over the past 50, 75, or even 100 years. But that is not relevant information if your investment timeframe is only 10 or 20 years.

Start saving in your 20s and you'll probably be on easy street by the time you reach age 60 – simply because you have so many years to unfold that plan. Retirees do not have that kind of extended window of opportunity for their investments to mature, though. It can be a grave mistake to apply the formulas that work for the majority of the younger investor population to those who face the challenge of preserving and growing their money during the later stages of life.

Anyone can buy assets and hold them as they experience the ups and downs of an increasingly turbulent market driven by forces including geo-politics, high-speed and high-volume trading algorithms, and domestic, global, and industry-specific economic cycles. Buy and hold long enough and you'll come out on top because buying is easy. Anybody can do it, and you don't even need a stock broker. But the hardest lesson to learn is when and why to sell and convert assets into liquid cash.

Just ask anyone who bought real estate properties in the early 2000s and then woke up to the nightmare of a market where nobody was interested in buying those assets. Putting your capital at risk without being rewarded is a serious pitfall when you no longer have the advantage of being able to live through several decades of market cycles. This is why I usually recommend a strategy where the dividends are high enough to offset that risk. Often times retirees put their money at risk in the market with the only hope for growth are the gains in the market. 'Hope' is a variable that doesn't belong in a retiree's portfolio. If you are in the market and exposing your retirement to the risk of the portfolio (because you believe you have to or need to) then you need to be properly compensating for that risk. Growth alone doesn't cut it. If the market is correcting or maintaining a sideways path, be paid with dividends until growth is provided.

Turning to history for a lesson, we find that since the 1930s more than half of total return in the stock market can be attributed to dividends, while only around 48% is from price appreciation. Dividends actually account for 100 percent of the returns in the S&P 500 between 2000 and 2012, as the markets experienced unpredictable swings.

That's because companies that pay steady dividends tend to be more stable, and their stock prices are usually less volatile. Younger investors who can afford to risk their cash on growth companies often find dividend stocks boring, because they don't provide extreme highs. Of course neither do they pose the threat of extreme downward moves. That makes them especially attractive and appropriate for a retiree, who is smart enough to invest in a tactical manner than preserves gains while also leveraging the compound yields that dividend payments offer.

When stocks lose value, cash is king – and since dividends are paid out in cash, high-quality dividend stocks have a built-in component to help preserve value. Dividends may also offer preferential tax advantages to investors.

To pay those dividends the company must have the cash on hand, too, which requires prudent corporate management. Companies these days are very adept at manipulating their earnings statistics and accounting metrics through creative bookkeeping practices, in order to promote their stock prices. Oftentimes they engage in this kind of smoke and mirrors game to the detriment of shareholders. But it is impossible for them to consistently pull hard cash out of the thin air. In order to raise enough case to continue paying dividends they must have real revenues and bankable profits. That's why so many companies with long histories of paying dividends – especially steadily increasing ones – are rock solid and keep making money through both bull and bear phases.

Retirees need to incorporate a strong defensive element into their investment strategies too. Because without that kind of proactive planning they open themselves up to negative repercussions that occur when they do not have time to recover from a loss and recoup their finances. Many asset allocation devotees say that the answer is to buy bonds to offset the losses posed if stock prices collapse. But history has proved them wrong before. Sometimes when stock prices fall bonds simultaneously lose value, especially when there is great uncertainty in the markets and investors retreat to the sidelines – or into traditional hard assets such as gold and cash.

Historically, bull markets like the one we are now enjoying last about five years. Already the current one has entered year number six, however, and many market observers are reminding investors that bear markets always follow bullish ones.

Another foreboding example of what astute analysts are watching is the rather unsettling divergence between the Dow Jones Industrial Average and the lesser known Russell 2000 index. While the more popular indices like the Dow and S&P are hitting new historical highs, the Russell 2000 (which is comprised of smaller cap stocks) has begun to move in the opposite direction. Usually when that happens it is a red flag that signals that the bull market has reached the end of its run. But no matter how you study the numbers or how much of an expert you are at predictions, nobody can ever time the markets. Trying to do so is a surefire way to expose yourself to more unwanted risk, because no alarm bells go off to notify anyone before the markets shift. What you can do, though, quite accurately in fact, is measure your own risk tolerance and use that as a reliable guide and protective mechanism.

An insightful question to ask, for instance, is how will your retirement portfolio hold up under a correction of 10 or 15 percent? Do you have time left to recover from a serious crash that could result in losses of 20 to 40 percent? Those happen, as you will recall if you were involved in the stock market during the implosion in 1987, the "dot-com" bust of the early 2000s, or the global market meltdown of the more recent Great Recession. What is your comfort level and how much loss can your lifestyle afford before your retirement is in jeopardy? Those are the questions your financial planner and investment strategy need to adequately address.

One of the most risk adverse investors in history is Warren Buffett, whose approach to investing has allowed him to avoid severe losses while taking advantage of bear markets as a prime buying opportunity. He understands that risk allocation is the key, because if you can earn profits and then hold on to them you'll succeed. Rather than attempting to time the markets, investors such as Buffett rely instead on tactical management of their portfolios. He always takes a strong and balanced position so that they are not overexposed to market surprises but still has the flexibility to take full advantage of rare buying or profit-taking opportunities.

In a perfect world, the financial markets would be entirely transparent and without mysteries. In this imperfect one, we have financial markets reliant on high-speed trading and dark pools, both of which are imperfectly understood. Thanks to the bestselling Flash Boys: A Wall Street Revolt and other journalistic efforts, the public is more aware of them.

While alternative trading platforms such as IEX (founded by Brad Katsuyama, the central figure of Flash Boys) have emerged, the anxieties remain. Reforms to U.S. market structure take time – often, too much time. At present, as Flash Boys notes, major U.S. exchanges such as the NYSE and NASDAQ have sold prime access to their premises to high-frequency trading networks, giving that software a clear competitive advantage over fund managers and individual investors.

Q: Does high-speed trading hurt individual investors? Lewis (who used to work on Wall Street before becoming a journalist) contends that the machinations of high-frequency trading amount to "computerized scalping" with the small investor paying a "tax" of half a percent (or less) per trade. Some economists and consumer advocates have argued for a "Robin Hood" tax in response – a surcharge of 3 basis points on financial transactions, with revenue generated going to the Treasury and helping to whittle down the federal budget deficit. Other economists call that a lousy idea, saying that taxing trading would only amount to a tax on savings – any such levy would ding the small investor even more, they argue, and Wall Street firms would just hunt for ways to avoid the tax.

Other stock market analysts feel high-speed trading helps investors more than it hurts them, citing what they see as improved market liquidity and referring to the reduction in bid-ask spreads (the differential between what buyers want to pay for a stock versus what sellers believe it is worth). Since the mid-1990s, bid-ask spreads have narrowed from the vicinity of 90 basis points to about 3 basis points as an effect of such trading networks.

Q: How long will high-speed trading rule the markets? It doesn't really "rule" them at the moment, but it does account for about half of all U.S. market volume right now. If it is any comfort, the percentage of market activity conducted via algorithmic trading platforms declined by 10% in the current bull market (according to The Atlantic, it went from 61% in 2009 to 51% in 2012).

Q: What really goes on in dark pools? For the uninitiated, dark pools are the private trading platforms maintained by banks. We can't see what goes on inside these private trading venues, as they aren't public exchanges like the NYSE or NASDAQ. The SEC is finally investigating them – its current chair, Mary Jo White, thinks they "risk seriously undermining" the credibility and validity of stock prices.

Dark pools account for about 40% of equities trading in America, and they aren't policed nearly as much as the public exchanges. As there are 11 public stock exchanges in this country compared to 40+ dark pools, there seems to be a sizable amount of trading going on behind closed doors.

Brad Katsuyama, the former Royal Bank of Canada trader who spearheaded the reform movement chronicled in Flash Boys, plans to introduce a pricing system that will let most banks and brokerages trade on the IEX platform for free – a move that might encourage them to get out of the dark pools (where they face no fees that they would ordinarily incur for trading on the public exchanges) and bring more of their trading into the light. But even IEX currently operates as a dark pool – though it plans to register with the Securities and Exchange Commission soon and become a full-fledged exchange – and its proposed pricing system would explicitly favor brokerages over individual investors.

Will trading ever truly be transparent? It would be naïve to think so. And until it is, I won't place my client's hard earned money at risk without some sort of protection by using tactical management.

If you have some tactical management in your portfolio you may not get all the upside of the market but not exposing yourself to all the losses will many times put you ahead of the game. Take these hypothetical numbers as an example:

	Tactical	Non-Tactical
Year 1	+10%	+36%
Year 2	+6%	+8%
Year 3	+8%	-20%
Average Return	+8%	+8%
Annualized Return	+8%	+5.4%
Needed in year 4	0	16%

As you can see, the tactical management portfolio underperformed in each year there was growth. Yet by reacting and not predicting, the portfolio was moved into cash in year 3 and didn't suffer the 20% loss as the non-tactical side did. Each portfolio had the same average return yet in year 4 the non-tactical portfolio needs a 16% return just to equal the tactical side.

Keep in mind that the markets often appear the healthiest at times when they are actually the weakest. Maybe you've had the misfortune and experienced the tragedy of losing a friend or colleague who seemed perfectly healthy, but then suffered a heart attack – seemingly out of the blue. The same can happen in the markets. They may look healthy to outside observers, while the fundamentals are actually terrible. The top 10% of the S&P 500 can carry the average and it may be going higher. However the majority of the companies may be trending lower. This can be a signal that the future may not be as rosy as you may see in the press. Think about all of the sudden corrections and devastating bear markets in history. Before the markets reversed direction there were plenty of reasons for optimism and many ways to justify a continued upward surge. But looks can be deceiving, which is why the smart money depends not on subjective points of view but on technical models that are reviewed daily to watch market momentum. Meteorologists don't just look at the sky or feel their creaky bones to predict the weather – otherwise they'd be out of a job. They use data models and fine-tuned instruments to stay several days or weeks ahead of impending storms or to see improved conditions on the horizon. That's the kind of financial planning a retiree needs, particularly today – when holding on to the wealth they have worked so hard to accumulate – is absolutely vital to a sustainable and stress-free retirement. So if you are being sold a bill of goods by your financial planner that is based on asset allocation, remember that the value of those assets is subject to change – at a moment's notice.

So, what exactly is tactical management? There are three categories that fall under this category and I only agree with one of them for retirees. The first are target date funds. These types of funds have an end date which is supposed to coordinate with your intended retirement date. The idea is the fund usually has a certain mix of stocks, bonds, and cash to meet the risk tolerance of the average investor who plans on retiring when the fund matures. As that date approaches, the fund will change the investment mix to reduce the risk. This usually means investing more in bonds and cash. They made a huge splash when they first entered the market. And I suppose if investors don't want to choose their own investments, not sure how to alter the blend as retirement approaches and won't hire an Investment Advisor then it isn't a bad option. However, if you examine the investment mix and when the investments begin moving into bonds and cash, it varies widely from target fund to target fund. So, in a sense it is tactical but falls short for many retirees.

You can see the difference in allocation mix in the Table 1.

Table 1 – Target Date Fund Current Allocations

Fund	Stock (%)	Bond (%)	Other (%)	Cash (%)
Fidelity Freedom 2020	20	40	-	40
Schwab Target 2020	25	68	-	7
T. Rowe Price Retirement 2020	20	80	-	-

USAA Target Retirement 2020	30	70	-	-
Vanguard Target Retirement 2020	30	65	-	5
iShares S&P Target Date 2020**	31.5	68.2	-	0.4

Source: Morningstar Inc - Data as of 8/31/2012.

In 2008, target date funds were criticized for incurring larger losses than investors perceived they would incur. Four years later, a study by ING found that a large number of investors still don't understand the very basics of target date funds ("Target Date Funds Misunderstood," April 2012 AAII Journal; available at AAII.com). According to the study, just 44% of investors surveyed knew that a target date fund's allocation is designed to automatically change over time. In my research, I've seen target funds that are three years away from their intended retirement date and have 50% allocation in stocks. I understand that retirees can sometimes need a significant allocation in stocks to ensure that their portfolio grows at a rate faster than inflation but, in my opinion, that won't be accomplished with target date funds.

The second type of tactical management is where the manager has free range to buy and sell within various types of investments in order to maximize the upside and limit the downside. This type of tactical management is more an attempt to time the market and outperform benchmarks. And this can often lead to a free range of possible investments including derivatives that can add unnecessary risk to a retiree's portfolio. I could site countless research articles illustrating that timing the market is impossible. After you pay the manager, the transaction costs and fund costs, it's virtually impossible for the fund to beat the benchmark. Usually the benchmark is the 'market' which is defined by the S&P500.

The third type and the only type I use are tactical funds that have a certain investment philosophy and will only maintain that mix when fully invested or a mix of that investment and cash or cash substitutes (Treasuries, etc.). They will have a certain percentage in the investments when their research shows the market is on an uptrend and move in to cash or cash substitutes when it shows a down trend. But once fully invested they do not have free range to invest in whatever the manager(s) feel might work. They maintain a certain type of investment mix. So, I can invest in the best way for my clients and I know there will be no deviation from that philosophy. The only change is when the fund is in reaction mode and shifting money to cash to protect my clients from the downside.

In order to find these types of mutual funds, you'll need to search whatever database you feel comfortable using. I've cited Fidelity and Vanguard before in this book and will do so again for providing free information for various mutual funds. You could also get a membership at Morningstar.com in order to take it further where various financial reporters will offer opinions on certain funds. Unfortunately, you'll find that some of these types of funds have minimums that are required to purchase. An advantage of working with an Advisor like myself that has a large client base is those minimums are usually waived.

If you want smooth sailing during your retirement years, then embrace a risk allocation approach to investing instead. Risk is the real enemy to the portfolio of anyone over the age of 50 or older. Control that and you can put the power of investing back where it belongs – within your own hands for a stable and rewarding retirement.

BONUS: Call or email now to subscribe to my monthly print newsletter. It's written just for retirees and I always pack it full of my latest research. Plus travel destinations, insurance tips and much more. Call the office at (248) 785-3734 or email us at newsletter@bridgeriverllc.com and provide your name and address. Let us know you saw this bonus in my book and the first year subscription is FREE.

CHAPTER 4 - EXECUTIVE ORDER NO. 6102

STEP THREE - You may have heard the saying, "In Washington, 'Trillion' is the new 'billion'. Trillion is such a large number that it's hard for most people to grasp. Even when I read that it's more than all the stars in the sky and every grain of sand in all the beaches of the world. I often ask audience members in my seminars if they know how long it will take if I stood in front of them and looked at my watch for 1 trillion seconds. The answer is 32,000 years.

Yet, as I write this, the U.S. is over 17 Trillion in debt and we've printed over three trillion in new dollars to keep liquidity in the market and continue to print money at the rate of 35 billion a month until October of 2014. Many experts and economists agree that the best way to protect your wealth from the ravages of inflation is to hold tangible assets. Those that you hold in your possession. Of course, when I mention tangible assets, most people think of gold. And while gold is a decent hedge against inflation, it isn't the best. Over 14 periods where inflation exceeded 4%, gold only outperformed in 8 of those periods. And I'll only briefly mention the fact at one point in history gold *was* confiscated so own actual gold at your own risk. In fact, America has actually seen four different gold confiscations, the last of which occurred during the Great Depression in 1933 with Executive Order No. 61202. President Franklin D. Roosevelt, in an attempt to control the monetary and banking crisis associated with the Great Depression, confiscated all privately owned gold in the United States (See the appendix for the actual executive order – scary stuff!). From 1933 until 1974, US. Citizens could not legally own gold. And although the right to own gold was restored in 1974, the language has remained that the Secretary of Treasure can demand individuals surrender their gold. The law is clear, private ownership of gold is a privilege to be enjoyed at its discretion rather than as a right. So, gold is not the best tangible asset to own to fight inflation. Mostly because it's a known currency replacement and easily valued so confiscation is always possible again.

So, what is better and still tangible and highly unlikely to be confiscated? Collectibles and more specifically high grade rare coins. Before you write this off as a crazy idea and skip to the next chapter, give me a few pages to change your mind. If my suggestion of owning tangible assets that you can touch and hold and are in high demand and can be highly valuable is crazy then think about this for a minute. What if I recommended an investment that had the following qualities?

1. You will never receive anything physical in return for your purchase.

2. The value of the investment is determined (and changes) every second of the business day. And also changes on nights and weekends yet its much less transparent and can drastically change the value on the next business day.

3. Various third party auditing firms verify the stability of the investment by examining the financials yet it is drastically open to interpretation and fraud has occurred because they are funded by the firm they are auditing.

4. The market this investment trades in has been said to suffer from mental illness (an actual quote from Warren Buffet). Its high one day and low the next. You can never predict it and it seems to fluctuate dramatically without anyone knowing exactly why.

5. The investment can be manipulated by large institutions in order to further their own goals.

Sounds pretty crazy, right? If you have ever invested in a stock, mutual fund, ETF or variable annuity then you have gladly accepted these terms. So, let's change our thinking and consider that tangible assets might be a good fit for a retiree's portfolio.

First off, rare coins were specifically mentioned in the infamous executive order as an EXCLUSION. Determining the appropriate compensation for collectibles such as high grade rare coin collections is a logistical impossibility. To determine the fair value collector-by-collector and coin-by-coin makes it highly unlikely. And secondly, and probably more important, high grade rare coins have the highest degree of correlation to inflation to any other investments. What this means is when inflation goes up there is a very high probability that the value of your high grade rare coins will go up as well.

The first thing to understand is collecting high grade rare coins is not a fad. They've been collected for more than 2000 years. Mostly because the introduction of currency and a monetary policy is considered one of the most incredible things brought to our society tracked back to the first paper banknotes issued in Europe in 1661. Because of this, people have always considered coins as a much sought after artifact of history. The U.S. Mint says 100 million Americans collect coins and there is constant pressure on the high end of rare coins (and the only ones I recommend to my clients) increasing demand. There are simply not enough rare coins to go around.

So, the demand is high but what exactly makes a rare coin valuable? The value is essentially predicated on two factors: rarity and quality. Rarity is determined by the number of coins existing in the same grade as determined by a numismatic auditing firm like NGC. Quality refers to the professionally assessed evaluation of the surface characteristics of a coin. Since 1986, the rare coin market, through the two major certification services, have utilized the Sheldon System, to classify the levels of preservation of rare coins. There are three key considerations in that process: surface preservation, luster, and strike.

Rare coins have a history of providing very nice returns in virtually all periods of economic growth, inflationary and otherwise. A study was conducted by Dr. Raymond Lombra of the economist department at Penn State University. In his study, Professor Lombra examined the performance of various investments, including gold and rare coins, over a quarter century ending in 2011. Here are some of his conclusions:

During the 25 year period studied, rare coins were a better diversifier than gold for a portfolio of stocks and bonds. Rare coins achieved substantial gains even during periods when the price of gold fell. For example, from 1988-1990, rare coins appreciated more than 100%, while the price of gold fell from $500 to $360.

The average annual return from rare coins was over 200% better than the average annual return of gold. The total return from rare coins in their best year was nearly 100% better than the return from gold in its best performing year. The total return from rare coins in their best three-year period was almost 100% better than the return from gold in its best three-year period.

Cycle after cycle, rare coins have made their owners more than proud; they've made them wealthy. Average growth in the normal 4-year up cycle exceeds 40% per year. During the last growth cycle, (1986-1990), coins went up approximately 195% in those four years. The largest cycle ever was the 1974-1982 market in which coins went up between 500% to over 1000% in only four years. All of this is full documented, historical fact. Rare coins are also private to buy or sell. There is no requirement that any branch of government be notified of any transaction involving the buying and selling of rare coins. They can be bought or sold anonymously with proceeds sent to anyone, anywhere in the free world. Heirs can and will avoid probate, state taxes and federal taxes. Literally millions of dollars can be passed on through this medium. I will often recommend a rare coin collection for my clients that are physicians, dentists, attorneys, executives and any party of wealth that needs shielding against malpractice and other litigation. No one knows you own them unless you wish them to. They can't be located by any conventional means.

Let's get back to some basics regarding rare coins. In order to do this, I'm going to reprint a special report from the coin expert I deal with. His name is Anthony Scirpo and is President of Farmington Valley Rare Coin & Investment Company, Inc. He can be reached at

860-379-3435. The idea of investing in high grade rare coins is scary for most and Anthony lives and breathes rare coins. Between my mentor, Curt Whipple and myself, we've known him for over 14 years and he has helped our clients immensely.

GETTING COMFORTABLE WITH RARE COINS
Anthony M. Scirpo

There's nothing strange or unusual about the certified rare coin asset. Please note that I said 'certified'. A certified rare coin preferably authenticated and graded by the Numismatic Guaranty Corporation of America (NGC), the market's leading certification service should make you very comfortable. Comfortable because the numismatic grade of every NGC encapsulated specimen is absolutely guaranteed. That guarantee is cash-backed by the certification service, NGC.

1. What is the NGC guarantee?
   NGC warrants that every rare coin specimen that they laboratory certify (every coin that they encapsulate in a tamper-proof, state-of-the-art, hologram-protected holder), is guaranteed as to the coin's numismatic grade, i.e., MS-65 or Proof-65, etc., or whichever grade that the service, NGC, states that it is.
2. What does the NGC guarantee men to our clients?

In a word, everything. A coin's value is substantially determined by its grade; hence, the certification service plays a vital role by "leveling the playing field." This market didn't have certification services until 1986. Prior thereto, a coin's grade, and its value, was governed by subjective opinion from whichever rare coin professional that you chose to do business with. Thankfully, this is a thing of the past. Yes, you can still buy uncertified coins, but today no investor or investor-collector does that. Why flirt with danger? A one point difference in grade can mean thousands of dollars...even tens of thousands of dollars of difference in price. You don't need someone's opinion; you want the guaranteed knowledge that your rare coin collection will always price out in accordance with the assigned grade of the coin.

Note: Neither the certification service or Farmington Valley Rare Coin guarantees the rare coin market. The rare coin market is definably cyclical, which means that the price of a coin, like that of a stock, will rise or fall with market conditions. As an example, coins that I'm selling in today's market for $3,000 to $4,000 were formerly priced at $7,500.00+ to $10,000+ during our last high cycle. Please remember...the coin market high cycle only comes along every 7 years or so, sometimes longer. Accordingly, it would be in everyone's best interests to diversify now and buy in at or near today's lower market prices levels.

3. Tangible or Intangible? What's best for my clientele? For me? Actually, both. The dictates of sound judgment and proper financial planning require that all of us have a diversified market basket of investments in our investment portfolios. It's a matter of historical fact that no one investment or class of investments is good for all times and all seasons. Over the last decade plus, we've seen the DOW go up significantly, only to be seriously humbled...so clearly, stocks don't go up in value forever. Mutual Funds generally fare in accordance with the stock market because mutual funds are merely collections of stocks, but will they keep going up forever? Only the most naïve of us would answer yes to this question. In fact, based on my research, and in anticipation of monetization of the debt, owning to massive government borrowing and overspending, the tables are not only due to be turned, but they definitely will be. Stocks will significantly decline; and in an inflationary run-up sustain heretofore "unthinkable" losses. Typically, when financial tides change, tangible assets come into serious favor as they did in 1979 through 1983. Remember the sale of several Van Gogh's in excess of $60 million per? Did you know that the top end of the rare coin market was the number one ranked investment during this same period and that this market's stellar results were reported in the Wall Street Journal? It was a time of SERIOUS INFLATION.

4. Why diversify? Diversification is the only game in town, but you can't diversify with just stocks, bonds, or mutual funds, irrespective of the nature, service or product that they represent. Stock are stocks...they're all subject to the wiles and whims of Wall Street Brokerages and that market's psychology; same applies to mutual funds. This is why tangible assets are necessary...**absolutely necessary**. Hence, better financial planners diversify and do so on a timely basis. The rare coin asset is a common sense, uncomplicated investment...and without a doubt, it's also the most interesting of all investments, replete with the romance and adventure of history.

5. The future...

   I can't predict the future. I'm guided by the past and influenced by my own exhaustive study of geo-political economics. I am also influence by independent, totally objective, economic forecasts from true experts. I then combine all of this information with my knowledge of law and monetary science; and attempt to give you the best forecast possible. By law, I cannot guarantee my own forecasts, or the rare coin market or any market...and I never have. We must all make our own decisions, but no matter what, it makes no sense to be without top quality, certified American rare coins. It's hard to deny a 50 year+ track record and harder still to justify and failure to diversify in light of the inflationary conflagration that we will be facing. It's not a question of 'if'. Only when…and 'when' is coming.

CHAPTER 5 - REAL ESTATE HEDGE

STEP FOUR - Over time, real estate has offered an effective hedge against inflation. So much so I regularly advise my clients to hold off on downsizing the home they live in for as long as possible. But for this chapter, I'll be writing in regards to commercial real estate. It's an even better hedge, and for reasons I'll explain soon, a better investment for retirees. Its historical performance supports this. Over long-term periods, commercial real estate outpaced inflation nicely. And even in short term periods the relation is close enough to make a strong argument to have commercial real estate in your portfolio.

TIAA-CREF demonstrated this by constructing hypothetical portfolios of commercial real estate, U.S. Treasury securities, stocks and bonds. Using 5,000 random starting points between 1978 and 2010 for hypothetical portfolios and calculated returns over five-year holding periods. In 83% of the portfolios, commercial real estate returns beat inflation. For portfolios, the average outperformance was 7.17%.

So, why does commercial real estate tend to do well in inflationary times? It tends to have specific characteristics that can help them keep pace with inflation. Most important is the structure of leases. Rent is usually brought to current levels when a lease is up for renewal. The rent on shorter term leases can catch up to inflation quicker but even in longer term leases there are step-ups to allow for increases that are actually tied to inflation. Even certain expenses are passed on to the tenant so commercial real estate owners aren't absorbing the increases.

Property values can be another factor. Everyone, I'm sure, can agree that interest rates will eventually be rising as they have been on a downward trend for more than ten years. Rising interest rates force property values down. At the same time, the economy is showing signs of growth and that can increase net operating income. The more net operating income generated by a property, the greater the odds that the property will also appreciate in value matching or exceeding inflation, even if interest rates increase.

This relationship is most powerful when supply conditions are tight. If the supply is high then it becomes a 'buyer's market'. It's harder for commercial real estate owners to negotiate favorable terms.

However, when the supply is down, the power to create inflation protected terms shifts to the owners. The strategy here is to buy real estate where the supply is low and demand is high. As I write this, I have the perfect way to do this. It may shift at some point but for now the investment is looking to support the 10,000 baby boomers that are retiring every day. I can't think of an investment that will have a higher demand than that.

There are many ways you can invest in real estate and more specifically, commercial real estate. You can buy property or you can purchase a stock of a company that builds or owns properties. You can also purchase an ETF or mutual fund that buys and sells companies that are in the real estate business. And lastly, you can purchase into a real estate investment trust (REIT). Buying a commercial property is expensive and not feasible for most retirees. So, your left with mutual funds and REITs. A REIT is simply a company that owns, and often manages, income producing property. It is important to be aware of the essential difference between a REIT and a real estate mutual fund. Real estate mutual funds are 'open-ended'. This means that you can redeem the value of the shares at any time. That means that whether or not the fund has the money on hand or not, if redemption is requested the fund has to comply. The result of this is that when markets cool, investors want out, and the fund finds itself carrying a heavy liquidation event. Where do they get the money? They sell some property in an already depressed market. REITs on the other hand are not open ended. They are 'closed-ended':

X number of units are issued and traded on the stock exchange. Sure, they rise and fall depending on what's happening in the marketplace with the value of the properties in the trust but the REIT has no obligation to redeem the units. Just like any other stock market investment the REIT holder sells it in the market for whatever it will bring. For these reasons, I prefer the stability of the REIT over that of a mutual fund. But we can't stop there because you must drill down to an even more specific type of REIT to find the type that I believe are better for those in or near retirement. As previously discussed, you can purchase into a REIT that is listed on the exchange, meaning there are potentially buyers and sellers, so liquidity is increased but you're exposed to market volatility. Or you can buy into a REIT that is non-traded. As I've mentioned before, my strategies for clients involve getting as much of a return as possible while keeping risk as low as possible. Unfortunately, the stock market and risk go hand in hand. So, if I can avoid the market, I will. This is one avenue of your portfolio where you can do just that. I prefer the non-traded for one less connection to the volatility of the market.

There is a tradeoff when purchasing a non-traded REIT. When an investment is traded on the market you have buyers and sellers. This is a double edge sword. Those same buyers and sellers that provide liquidity also cause volatility as they are free to sell on any whim. And don't forget, we aren't only discussing an investor who decides to sell in his/her 401k or IRA. I'm also talking about the hedge funds and high speed computers that buy and sell millions of shares at a time that add to the volatility. When you own a non-traded REIT you give up some of that liquidity. You don't have a large exchange of willing buyers and sellers. For most of my clients, we can plan accordingly and it becomes less of an issue. I will note however that this is another important distinction between those advisors that get paid a commission to put their clients in a non-traded REIT and those that do not. As discussed previously, as a Registered Investment Advisor, I do not get paid a commission to put my clients in this type of investment. Therefore, the cost to purchase is less for my clients and the liquidity is greatly increased. If you remember my discussion on how liquidity is affected when investing in a variable annuity in the 'Social Security' chapter then the same applies here. If an insurance company is paying the advisor a commission then liquidity is greatly decreased as the insurance company doesn't want to pay the advisor a commission and then have you withdraw all your money six months later. As a fee based advisor, we aren't paid a commission so there is no decrease in liquidity and usually no surrender charges (for a bare bones product). Same goes with a non-traded REIT. If you deal with a commissioned advisor you will be paying more per share and your liquidity will be much lower than a fee based advisor who does not get paid a commission.

There are certain restrictions on most non-traded investment vehicles or 'alternative investments' that only allow access to certain investors. And depending on where the investment is held (the custodian) they also may place more restrictions. Some restrictions may include such requirements like the investment must be purchased inside an IRA. And the value can't be more than 60% of the total value of the IRA. The large majority will at least require the investor(s) have a net worth (excluding home, home furnishings and automobiles) of at least $70,000 and gross income of at least $70,000; or have a net worth (excluding home, home furnishings and automobiles) of at least $250,000 or such higher suitability as may be required by each state (see Appendix 3).

As mentioned before the REITs I favor now support those 10,000 baby boomers that are retiring every day. I can't think of a better supply and demand issue that favors my clients. The REITs I prefer have a diversified portfolio of medical office buildings, hospital, assisted living and other healthcare facilities. This is perfect as the leading crest of baby boomers started turning 65 in 2011. They very well may have parents in their 80s and 90s and the majority will need to be cared for. By 2050, 1/5th of the US population will be over 65. And the population of those over age 85 is increasing even faster. By 2050 this demographic will triple. And as compared to the age bracket of 45 to 64, those that are 65 and older have a 77% increase in healthcare expenditure.

Once you become a shareholder, the intent of a REIT is to pay consistent monthly distributions from rents paid by tenants on properties they acquire. As I write this, the average is around 7%. The strategy is to own a set value of properties. Once they purchase enough, the strategy is to 'target a liquidity event'. In essence, the

REIT now has an attractive portfolio that can be sold to a publically traded REIT. This liquidity event is usually between three to eight years from their start date. Investors can either choose to stay in the public REIT and continue to receive the dividends or sell the shares on the open market if liquidity is needed or the shares sell at an attractive price. In the past, my clients have been handsomely rewarded for investing in the REIT while in the non-traded stage but there are no guarantees.

These types of investments, along with other sophisticated investment vehicles can get very confusing. It comes down to performing your own due diligence and trusting your advisor.

CHAPTER 6 - PUTTING IT ALL TOGETHER

Now that you have an effective inflation plan, it's time to put it all together. You'll want to start with a financial calculator or spreadsheet (if you're really handy). Something that you can input your retirement savings, pensions, social security and the retirement income needed along with inflation rates and cost of living adjustments for pensions. The figure you're looking for is the rate of return needed from your portfolio in order for your retirement portfolio to last to whatever age you desire. A good place to start is to search the internet for 'calculators to outlive your money'. I use a system called 'Red Blue Green'. It was created by Curt Whipple, an advisor in Plymouth, Michigan. Many advisors use this software and it's very powerful. I use it like a 'retirement report card' with my clients. If I plug in all the necessary numbers it creates a spreadsheet showing exactly the rate of return I need my clients portfolio to perform at to make sure they don't outlive their money. If we have set up a portfolio to match the rate of return that the report card tells us we need, then we know we are on track. Every time I meet with my clients we review the report card to make necessary adjustments. We may update the inflation rate or if a particular investment has performed better or worse than we expected we'll make adjustments. In the end, if the report illustrates that we need, say $346,754, in our retirement accounts to stay on track and we have that amount or more, then we've made it one more year knowing we won't outlive our money.

The same goes for whatever calculator or spreadsheet you find online. Input all the necessary figures it requests including a hypothetical return to calculate what balance it requires to illustrate your retirement money lasting. Once it shows that it lasts to the desired age you would like then you have the two most important figures. The first is the rate of return you need to outlive your money and the size of your portfolio required to do so. If you're portfolio size is nowhere in the ballpark then you may need to adjust how you planned on living in retirement. If it's close enough to where you can adjust your rate of return to make it last until a desired age then that's where you need to start.

Once you have that rate of return needed then you need to combine the investments in this book and others you wish to hold to match that rate. If it sounds complicated, it is. And I know that sounds self-serving if I make it feel like you can't do this on your own. The problem is, I actually feel that most can't do it on their own. What I do is not rocket science and yes, some are more than capable of investing on their own for retirement. But in retirement if you're investing and withdrawing from your accounts, it's a whole different ball game. It's a lot like when I read my wife's medical journals. Like any profession, they too have their own language and words that you don't hear outside of the medical world. I can read a simple article about myocardial infarction and won't understand one bit. Every sentence they use words I've never seen or heard before. I'd need a medical dictionary to translate. And after finishing the article, I might understand it but couldn't do much with the knowledge without a lot more work.

Let me show you an example to really drive the point home how it's different when you're retired and withdrawing money than it is when you are still in the accumulation phase. There are two phases of your investing lifespan. The accumulation phase and the distribution phase. Compare it to a mountain where the upside is the accumulation phase the peak is your flag when you choose to retire and then the downside is the distribution phase. And 'downside' sounds as if I'm looking at retirement as the 'downside' of life. As most retirees know, it quite the opposite as I joke with my monthly newsletter heading of "Retirement Monthly - Goodbye Tension, Hello Pension". However, the downside does accurately reflect that during a market correction of any significance would cause you to 'fall' down the mountain. At age 75, it might be more difficult to recover and get back up the mountain than if you were 35 on the accumulation side.

On the following page, note the columns under 'Example Index" in figure 1. It illustrates your ending balance if you began at age 65 with $500,000 in your retirement portfolio during the accumulation stage. This means you can take on more risk and be fully invested in the stock market. The yearly returns are hypothetical but developed in order to generate an average rate of return of approximately 8% over a 30 year period. This is the rate of return most experts will tell you is the average yearly return of the stock market. In the beginning you had some really great years with some really not so great years at the end. After 30 years you would end up with $4,980,555. Not bad, right?

Now, let's look at the columns under "Example Index Reversed" in figure 1. Everything is the same except I flipped the returns. If you'll notice the yearly returns under 'Example Index" start with 18%, 6%, 11%, 5%, 19%, etc.. Under "Example Index Reversed", those numbers are at the bottom. And at the bottom of the yearly return figures under "Example Index" are 23%, 27%, -12%, -

16%, 8%, etc. Under "Example Index Reversed", those numbers are at the top. What happens to the end of year value after 30 years? Nothing! Absolutely nothing. Instead of starting out with great returns in the beginning and ending with some terrible years we had the opposite occur and the end result didn't matter at all.

Accumulation
The "Upside" of the Mountain

		Example Index			Example Index Reversed		
Year	Age	Beginning Amount	Yearly Return	End Of Year Value	Beginning Amount	Yearly Return	End Of Year Value
1	65	$500,000	18%	$590,000	$500,000	8%	$540,000
2	66	$590,000	6%	$625,400	$540,000	-16%	$453,600
3	67	$625,400	11%	$694,194	$453,600	-12%	$399,168
4	68	$694,194	5%	$728,904	$399,168	27%	$506,943
5	69	$728,904	19%	$867,395	$506,943	23%	$623,540
6	70	$867,395	-5%	$824,026	$623,540	-15%	$530,009
7	71	$824,026	18%	$972,350	$530,009	22%	$646,611
8	72	$972,350	-6%	$914,009	$646,611	18%	$763,001
9	73	$914,009	18%	$1,078,531	$763,001	-12%	$671,441
10	74	$1,078,531	23%	$1,326,593	$671,441	20%	$805,729
11	75	$1,326,593	3%	$1,366,391	$805,729	14%	$918,532
12	76	$1,366,391	11%	$1,516,694	$918,532	-6%	$863,420
13	77	$1,516,694	-5%	$1,440,859	$863,420	18%	$1,018,835
14	78	$1,440,859	31%	$1,887,525	$1,018,835	12%	$1,141,095
15	79	$1,887,525	23%	$2,321,656	$1,141,095	-6%	$1,072,630
16	80	$2,321,656	-6%	$2,182,357	$1,072,630	23%	$1,319,335
17	81	$2,182,357	12%	$2,444,240	$1,319,335	31%	$1,728,328
18	82	$2,444,240	18%	$2,884,203	$1,728,328	-5%	$1,641,912
19	83	$2,884,203	-6%	$2,711,151	$1,641,912	11%	$1,822,522
20	84	$2,711,151	14%	$3,090,712	$1,822,522	3%	$1,877,198
21	85	$3,090,712	20%	$3,708,854	$1,877,198	23%	$2,308,953
22	86	$3,708,854	-12%	$3,263,792	$2,308,953	18%	$2,724,565
23	87	$3,263,792	18%	$3,851,274	$2,724,565	-6%	$2,561,091
24	88	$3,851,274	22%	$4,698,554	$2,561,091	18%	$3,022,087
25	89	$4,698,554	-15%	$3,993,771	$3,022,087	-5%	$2,870,983
26	90	$3,993,771	23%	$4,912,339	$2,870,983	19%	$3,416,470
27	91	$4,912,339	27%	$6,238,670	$3,416,470	5%	$3,587,293
28	92	$6,238,670	-12%	$5,490,030	$3,587,293	11%	$3,981,896
29	93	$5,490,030	-16%	$4,611,625	$3,981,896	6%	$4,220,809
30	94	$4,611,625	8%	$4,980,555	$4,220,809	18%	$4,980,555

All market returns are purely hypothetical and developed in order to generate an average rate of return of approximately 8% over the 30 year period. These rates are not to be construed as actual past performance or potential

Figure 1

What this helps to illustrate is the fact that when you are younger and still accumulating without the need for withdrawing money for income it doesn't really matter if there is a great or bad market in the beginning, the end or anywhere! The idea is just to be in the market with a diversified portfolio to match your risk tolerance. Any

Distribution/Withdrawals
The "Downside of the Mountain"

	Illustrated Index				Illustrated index reversed			
Age	Beginning Amount	Yearly Return	Annual Withdrawal	End of Year Value	Beginning Amount	Yearly Return	Annual Withdrawal	End of Year Value
65	$ 500,000	18%	$35,000	$ 555,000	$ 500,000	8%	$ 35,000	$ 505,000
66	$ 555,000	6%	$36,050	$ 552,250	$ 505,000	-16%	$ 36,050	$ 388,150
67	$ 552,250	11%	$37,132	$ 575,866	$ 388,150	-12%	$ 37,132	$ 304,441
68	$ 575,866	5%	$38,245	$ 566,414	$ 304,441	27%	$ 38,245	$ 348,394
69	$ 566,414	19%	$39,393	$ 634,640	$ 348,394	23%	$ 39,393	$ 389,132
70	$ 634,640	-5%	$40,575	$ 562,333	$ 389,132	-15%	$ 40,575	$ 290,187
71	$ 562,333	18%	$41,792	$ 621,761	$ 290,187	22%	$ 41,792	$ 312,237
72	$ 621,761	-6%	$43,046	$ 541,410	$ 312,237	18%	$ 43,046	$ 325,394
73	$ 541,410	18%	$44,337	$ 594,527	$ 325,394	-12%	$ 44,337	$ 242,010
74	$ 594,527	23%	$45,667	$ 685,601	$ 242,010	20%	$ 45,667	$ 244,745
75	$ 685,601	3%	$47,037	$ 659,132	$ 244,745	14%	$ 47,037	$ 231,972
76	$ 659,132	11%	$48,448	$ 683,188	$ 231,972	-6%	$ 48,448	$ 169,605
77	$ 683,188	-5%	$49,902	$ 599,127	$ 169,605	18%	$ 49,902	$ 150,233
78	$ 599,127	31%	$51,399	$ 733,458	$ 150,233	12%	$ 51,399	$ 116,862
79	$ 733,458	23%	$52,941	$ 849,213	$ 116,862	-6%	$ 52,941	$ 56,909
80	$ 849,213	-6%	$54,529	$ 743,731	$ 56,909	23%	$ 54,529	$ 15,470
81	$ 743,731	12%	$56,165	$ 776,814	$ 15,470	31%	$ 56,165	$ (35,899)
82	$ 776,814	18%	$57,850	$ 858,791	$ (35,899)	-5%	$ 57,850	$ (91,954)
83	$ 858,791	-6%	$59,585	$ 747,678	$ (91,954)	11%	$ 59,585	$ (161,654)
84	$ 747,678	14%	$61,373	$ 790,980	$ (161,654)	3%	$ 61,373	$ (227,877)
85	$ 790,980	20%	$63,214	$ 885,963	$ (227,877)	23%	$ 63,214	$ (343,502)
86	$ 885,963	-12%	$65,110	$ 714,537	$ (343,502)	18%	$ 65,110	$ (470,443)
87	$ 714,537	18%	$67,064	$ 776,090	$ (470,443)	-6%	$ 67,064	$ (509,280)
88	$ 776,090	22%	$69,076	$ 877,754	$ (509,280)	18%	$ 69,076	$ (670,026)
89	$ 877,754	-15%	$71,148	$ 674,943	$ (670,026)	-5%	$ 71,148	$ (707,672)
90	$ 674,943	23%	$73,282	$ 756,898	$ (707,672)	19%	$ 73,282	$ (915,412)
91	$ 756,898	27%	$75,481	$ 885,780	$ (915,412)	5%	$ 75,481	$ (1,036,663)
92	$ 885,780	-12%	$77,745	$ 701,741	$ (1,036,663)	11%	$ 77,745	$ (1,228,442)
93	$ 701,741	-16%	$80,077	$ 509,385	$ (1,228,442)	6%	$ 80,077	$ (1,382,225)
94	$ 509,385	8%	$82,480	$ 467,656	$ (1,382,225)	18%	$ 82,480	$ (1,713,506)

All market returns are purely hypothetical and developed in order to generate an average rate of return of approximately 8% over the 30 year period. These rates are not to be construed as actual past performance or potential

Figure 2

competent advisor can do that.

However, let's go one step further and see how everything changes in retirement. Look at figure 2 where I show the same data but it's set up where the investor is withdrawing $35,000 a year and it's increased to match a modest inflation rate of 3%. Under "Illustrated Index", how much is the ending value of this investors portfolio after 30 years with great gains in the market in the beginning and lousy returns at the end? Roughly $467,656. Not bad, after thirty years of withdrawing money and with an average return of 8% you ended up with roughly what you started with. Now let's continue to "Illustrated Index Reversed", where we once again flipped the returns to begin with lousy returns and ending with a very strong five year period. With everything else the same, what happens at age 81? You're broke! When you're young and accumulating, it doesn't matter when the returns happen in the market. If you are retired and withdrawing the market then it matters a lot. Getting nice market returns can still be very important when you're retired. Especially if your analysis shows that the balance of your retirement savings needs growth to be able to provide the retirement you desire. But at some point, *pure* growth needs to take a back seat to *smart* growth. Taking on too much risk when you're nearing or in retirement can be catastrophic.

The way I set up retirement accounts and the strategies I select to grow and withdraw my client's accounts in retirements is unique to every client and it depends on their risk tolerance, income needs and current and future income. All while structuring income to stay as low as possible to reduce income taxes. So, some retirees can do all this on their own but it requires a lot of research and unfortunately the internet can be the worst way to do so. It seems everyone has a hidden agenda and getting un-biased opinions is difficult.

I've covered some important topics and complicated investments and if you've made it this far, congratulations. Here are some options for your next step:

1. I am available to talk with anyone that would like to learn more about the strategies discussed in this book or more. You can call the office and schedule a 15 minute free phone consultation.

2. You can also call and request my monthly newsletter or by emailing newsletter@bridgeriverllc.com. We'll need your mailing address because this is a print newsletter, not email.

3. Visit my website at www.bridgeriverllc.com and click on the events tab to see where I'll be speaking next.

4. Visit www.nesteggspecialist.com to watch my free video series on strategies to make your retirement income last your lifetime.

5. For women, I've created a video series showing strategies at www.financetipsforwomen.com.

Thank you for taking the time to read my book. I congratulate you whether this is the first step in preparing for the coming inflation crisis or you are ready to take action. I think we are in unprecedented times and every retiree must take action. In retirement, mistakes are hard to overcome. Don't let inaction be your mistake. Take the necessary steps now to avoid the coming inflation crisis. As Theodore Roosevelt said, "In any situation, the best thing you can do is the right thing, the next best thing you can do is the wrong thing; the worst thing you can do is nothing."

APPENDIX 1 – THE ROTH IRA

So, what is a Roth IRA? A Roth IRA is an Individual Retirement Arrangement (TRA) that was established by the Taxpayer Relief Act of 1997. It is named for its main sponsor, the late Senator William Roth of Delaware. You may have noted that I wrote Individual Retirement Arrangement - not Account. You can have fun at parties quizzing your guests what the acronym is for IRA. Most will say Individual Retirement Account. Now you know why I am the life of most parties.

A Roth IRA, like the traditional IRA can hold various types of securities whether it's common stocks, mutual funds, notes, certificates of deposit, and real estate. As with all IRAs, there are specific eligibility and filing status requirements mandated by the Internal Revenue Service. An important figure for ROTH eligibility is your modified adjusted gross income (MAGI). In order to figure out your MAGI you first need to know what your AGI which is your total income (including wages, interest, income from retirement accounts, capital gains, and alimony received) less certain "adjustments". These adjustments include deductible IRA contributions, 401(K) or 403(b) contributions, alimony payments, health insurance premiums (if you're self-employed), moving expenses, and interest on student loans, among others. In order to arrive at your MAGI, add back income that you excluded.

For instance, interest income for series EE bonds, deductions that you may have claimed for student loan interest allowable tuition expensed, and any deduction that you may have claimed for a traditional IRA contribution. Also if you are receiving required minimum distributions from a traditional IRA to a Roth IRA do not count against your MAGI either. The limitations in your MAGI in order to contribute to a Roth are shown below.

	Full Contribution	Partial Contribution
Single and Married filing separately	Up to $113,999	$114,000 - $128,999
Married filing jointly or qualifying	Up to $180,999	$181,000 - $190,999

widow(er)

If you are married filing separately and lived with your spouse at any time during the year and make less than $10,000 you can make a partial contribution.   If you make $10,000 or more you are not allowed to make a contribution.

Once you determine if you can contribute to a Roth IRA you must determine your maximum contribution amount.   The amount is either the figures below or your modified adjusted gross income (MAGI), whichever is less.

	Age 49 and **Below**	**Age 50 and** **Above**
2014	$5,500	$6,500

Keep in mind these are total contribution amounts for Roth and traditional IRAs whether you put the full amount in a Roth or divide them equally between a Roth and a traditional IRA or any variation thereof.

For example, if you are single and have earned income of $10,000, you can contribute a maximum of $5,500 in 2014. However, if you are single and have earned income of $2,000, you can contribute only a maximum of $2,000 in 2014 ($2,000 is the lesser of $2,000 and $5,500).

The main difference between a Roth IRA and a traditional IRA are contributions to a Roth are not tax-deductible. Contributions may or may not be tax-deductible for a traditional IRA based on income limits. The tax savings for deducting a contribution to a traditional IRA can be calculated by multiplying the taxpayers' marginal tax rate by the amount contributed. Eligibility to contribute to Roth IRAs phases out depending on income as shown by the chart below.

So, should you take the tax write off now in a traditional IRA and forgo tax free withdrawals in a Roth? Many books much thicker than the one you are holding have tackled that question. It depends on many factors, most of which I will address. Another nice feature is contributions may be made to a Roth IRA even if you participate in a company plan, such as a 401(K). Contributions may be made to a traditional IRA is this circumstance, but they may not be tax deductible.

If you get that big promotion and your income increases past the limits, you can keep you Roth and your investments will remain tax-sheltered but you may or may not be able to continue contributions. Se 'Back Door Contributions' in the Conversion strategies chapter if this is an issue for you.

Withdrawals can be tax-free and even penalty free before the age of 59 ½ in a Roth IRA (this will be discussed in more detail in the next chapter). This differs from a traditional IRA where all withdrawals are taxed as ordinary income and a penalty applies for withdrawals before age 59 ½. In contrast, an account that is not tax deferred incurs capital gains on stocks or other securities held for at least a year. They would be taxed at a long term capital gain rate, which is currently 15%.

Another main difference between the Roth IRA and traditional IRA are required minimum distributions (RMDs). All tax-deferred retirement plans require withdraws based on age, even the Roth 401(k), a close relative. The age this requirement begins can vary from the norm of 70 ½ later depending on various factors. The Roth does not have any RMDs for you the owner.

If you don't need the money and want to leave it to your heirs, this is a great way to accumulate your investments tax free, however beneficiaries who inherit your Roth IRA are subject to the minimum distribution rules.

The year 2009 was the last year taxpayers needed to be concerned with the conversion limits of MAGI less than $100,000 in the year of conversion and not married filing separately. TIPRA 2005 eliminated the MAGI limit and filing status restriction on conversions starting in 2010. Now, anyone can convert traditional IRA funds to a ROTH.

Let's recap the four top benefits of owning a Roth IRA.

1. As far as leaving a tax-free legacy – there is little better.

2. Many believe tax rates are the lowest they will be for years to come. A Roth IRA locks in current tax rates.

3. Providing more choice. I purposely set up many of my clients' accounts with all three types of accounts: Traditional IRA, Roth, and taxable accounts. All provide different tax

structures that I can use to my clients advantage depending on income and tax requirements.

4. No required minimum distributions (RMDs). If you live long enough, the IRS will eventually get taxes due on the money accumulating in you traditional IRA. Not true with the Roth. There is no requirement to ever take money out of your Roth while you are still alive. For some, that alone is a game changer. Many of my clients are in higher tax brackets when they retire then in their working years. This is in large part due to RMDs.

By far, the vast majority of Roth IRA questions I get involve withdraws. There is a reason for this. With a traditional IRA, it is very straightforward. If you withdraw money, a portion of the withdraw is a return of your contributions and another portion are gains. There is no way to withdraw just the principal and there is no way to withdraw just the gains.

Of course, the return of your contributions may or may not be taxable depending on their source. For instance, if the IRA was formed by rolling over your company plan, such as a 401(k), that is all before-tax contributions, then the return of your contributions will be fully taxable. Same goes for any contributions to an IRA that you deducted. However, if you did not or could not deduct your traditional IRA contributions then these are return of contributions will not be taxable.

As you can see, traditional IRA withdraws aren't very complex but can require extensive record keeping. If you combine an IRA with after-tax and before-tax contributions, then you should be notifying the IRS via form 8606 detaining both. If you haven't done this then you can buy back your old tax returns from the IRS, using Form 4506, or you can order a free transcript of everything that's reported about you to the IRS, using form 4506-T. Included in your transcript is information from IRS Form 5498, which reports contributions you made to an IRA. Other resources are year-end statements from your IRA custodian.

My advice is usually to keep the IRAs separate. Company plan rollovers and deductible contributions can be one IRA and non-deductible contributions can be another IRA.

The reason withdrawing money from Roth IRAs is complicated lies in its tiered structure. There are three tiers in your Roth – Contributions, Conversions, and Earnings. There are two different taxes – income tax and the 10% penalty. And finally, there are two completely different five-year holding periods. Figure 1 shows the consequences of withdrawing.

Figure 1 – Withdraw order and consequences

1. Contributions   Always income tax and penalty free
2. Conversions   Always income tax free but only penalty free after 5 years or if you are over the age of 59 ½, whichever

comes first.

3. Earnings   In order to access earnings free of income taxes and penalties, you must meet 2 tests: You have owned ANY Roth for at least five years AND you are older than age 59 ½

As you can see each tier has its own requirements for withdraws to avoid taxes and/or penalties. The other notable aspect is a built in withdraw method. When you withdraw money it automatically comes from the top of the tier first. After that, tier 2 and so on.

I think the biggest misunderstood rule of the Roth IRA has to be that you **can** withdraw your contributions at any time penalty free. And because your contribution was already taxed they are tax-free also. It doesn't matter if your contribution has been in your Roth for five minutes or five years. There is no five-year rule for contributions. The confusion arrives when investors assume contributions and conversions are the same.

When you convert your traditional IRA or roll over your company plan (example 401(k)) to a Roth then you have conversion funds inside your Roth.

If you withdraw funds from your Roth and its conversion money then we are assuming that all contributions have been withdrawn or there were none. At one time, if you were younger than 59 ½ and you converted your traditional IRA to a Roth, you were able to withdraw your money tax-free. However, the IRS has since caught on to that loop hole and required a five-year seasoning limit. But once you reach 59 ½ you can withdraw conversion money tax and penalty free.

So, in summary, if you are less than 59 ½ years old, you have to wait at least five years or until you reach 59 ½ to access your conversion money income and penalty tax-free.

Say, you decide to roll three traditional IRAs into one Roth and you are withdrawing conversion funds. It is considered that you are withdrawing from the earliest conversion first and continuing in the order of conversion.

And finally, the earnings. This is the last tier to be touched when withdrawing money. And aside from the exceptions deemed penalty free from the IRS you are at no time allowed to withdraw earnings from your Roth penalty and tax-free before the age of 59 ½. Remember, this is supposed to be a retirement account.

In order to withdraw your earnings tax and penalty free you must meet two tests. You must be at least 59 ½ years of age and you must own any Roth for five years. The Roth you are withdrawing money from does not need to be seasoned for five years just any Roth that you own.

The exceptions to the 10% penalty are:

1. You had a "direct rollover" to your new retirement account.
2. You received a lump-sum payment but rolled over the money to a qualified retirement account within 60 days.
3. You were permanently or totally disabled.

4. You were unemployed and paid for health insurance premiums.

5. You paid for college expenses for yourself or a dependent.

6. You bought a house. (If you have not owned a home in the past two years then the IRS deems a purchase to be a first home and it's limited to $10,000).

7. You paid for medical expenses exceeding 7.5% of your adjusted gross income. (You do not need to itemize in order to claim the medical expense exception).

8. The IRS levied your retirement account to pay off tax debts.

In 2010, everyone could convert to a Roth IRA regardless of income thanks to the Tax Increase Prevention and Reconciliation Act of 2005 (TIPRA). Formerly, those with MAGI in excess of $100,000 could not qualify for a conversion. Additionally, married couples filing separately could not qualify to prevent income shifting.

So what exactly can you convert to a Roth? You can convert all or part of the assets from your own or an inherited employer-sponsored qualified pension, profit-sharing or stock-bonus plan, such as a 401(k) or 403(b), annuity plan, or a government-deferred compensation plan, such as a section 457. You can also convert your own (but not an inherited IRA), SEP IRA or a Savings Incentive Match Plan for Employees (SIMPLE). However you do have a SIMPLE for at least two years from the date of establishment before converting.

With the conversion from any of these tax-deferred accounts, as with a traditional IRA, the conversion amount is subject to income tax and this is referred to as the conversion tax. When I explain this to clients they usually run screaming out of my office. But it is important to keep your eye on the big picture. When you convert – you stop the tax clock. Usually paying the government early is a good thing and something I recommend.

And there is an option to do a tax-free conversion from a 401(k) if you have after-tax money and the plan will write two checks. If they will, then you can rollover the after-tax money with no pro-rata rule directly to a Roth and pay no taxes on the conversion.

The answer to 'Should you convert?' is both mathematical and political. For obvious reasons, I will only be tackling the mathematical portion. And, unfortunately, by the end of this chapter I will not have a definitive answer to the question of, 'Should you convert?' Certain circumstances are more slam dinks than others but there are a myriad of variables that can easily change the answer from 'yes' to 'no'. With Roth conversions some of the deciding factors are variables in which we do not know the answer.

For many investors, converting now is a good idea. For example, if an investor with a $20,000 tradition IRA makes $35,000 a year now and expects to have only $25,000 a year of income in retirement, he or she will probably be wise to go ahead and convert the IRA now and allow the tax-free growth to accumulate over time. But this scenario doesn't work for everyone. This general rule applies only to low or middle-income investors with smaller traditional IRA balances.

The six key variables to determining if a conversion is right for you are:

1. Traditional IRA balance – Smaller size accounts are usually a good idea. Larger accounts require more number crunching.

2. Time horizon – The more time you have to allow your new Roth to build tax deferred, the better.

3. Current and future income needs – It tends not to be a good idea if you need your new Roth for income. At least initially, anyway. If your time horizon allows the Roth to grow then it may make sense.

4. Current tax rate compared to projected tax rates – Keep in mind whether you plan to live in retirement in a state with lower income tax than you pay now-or, alternately, a state with higher income tax. This is obviously a main aspect of the number crunching.

5. Ability to pay the conversion tax with money other than your new Roth – All factors constant, it rarely makes sense to convert to a Roth if you do not have outside funds to pay the conversion tax.

6. Estate planning objectives – This will be discussed further in the Conversion Strategies chapter but if estate taxes are an issue it almost always makes sense to convert. Traditional IRA holders may pay estate taxes on money that will only be used

to pay income taxes at some point. So converting before death can make sense.

After identifying these 6 variables you can isolate three different types of Roth conversions:

Wealth Transfer conversions – because the Roth is a great tax-free present.

Strategy Based Conversions – to fit a specific need.

Recession Based – One that may make sense if your investments are down.

Each type is detailed with factors that make an ideal candidate.

Wealth Transfer Conversion

1. You have outside funds to pay the conversion tax.
2. You do not need the Roth for living expenses
3. You want to leave the Roth to your children or grandchildren
4. If you think you will be in the same or higher tax bracket in the future

Roth makes an ideal wealth transfer tool. Not only can the growth be exponential you are never required to withdraw any money during your lifetime. And although your beneficiaries will be required to withdraw money it will all be tax-free.

Keep in mind, if a charity will be the ultimate beneficiary of your Roth than it may not make sense to convert. The charity would not have to pay taxes on withdrawals, why should you?

Beyond that, it is a simple number crunching exercise to determine if it makes sense. You will need to figure out:

1. What your marginal tax rate is now compared to what you think it will be when you retire.
2. If you can pay the conversion tax with outside funds and
3. Your time horizon

I've performed these calculations enough to know that if you believe your future marginal tax bracket will be the same as it is now and if you do not have any outside funds to pay the conversion tax, then with all other factors constant, the conversion will have the identical economic outcome as if you did nothing as seen in Figure 2.

Figure 2 – Comparison using same tax bracket and outside funds

	Traditional IRA	Roth IRA
Less: Income tax on Roth IRA Conversion @ 25%		($25,000)
After-Tax Account Balance (Current)	$100,000	$75,000
Growth Factor	400%	400%

Pre-Tax Account Balance (Year 30)	$400,000	$300,000
Less: Income tax on IRA Withdrawal @ 25%	($100,000)	
After-Tax Account Balance (Year 30)	$300,000	$300,000

Things get more complicated when the variables of marginal tax rates change and using outside funds to pay the conversion tax change. There are many Roth conversion calculators on the Internet. Many are good, some are not so good. I have always preferred creating my own in an Excel spreadsheet. You can email me and I'll send you the one I use.

You simply plug in your traditional IRA value, your current marginal tax rate, and the marginal tax rate you believe will have when retired. The spreadsheet will assume you have enough in outside funds to pay the conversion tax and will automatically plug that number in. You also may change the pre-tax and after-tax growth rates you believe you might earn. The projections will show you the difference between converting and not converting. It will also project it over a 10, 20 and 30 year time horizon.

Strategy Based Conversion (will be covered more in the Conversion Strategies chapter)

1. If you have Net Operating Loss (NOL) carryforwards

2. Business losses

3. Deductions and Exemptions in excess of income

4. Charitable contribution carryforwards

5. Non-refundable tax credits

6. Income tax changes

7. Estate tax changes

An example of a strategy based conversion would be facing the possibility of losing favorable tax write-offs within the current year. This could be as the result of no taxable income due to carryforwards. A Net Operating Loss (NOL) carryforward would be a business loss that you weren't able to fully realize in one year. Therefore, you carry it over to subsequent year. Converting assets to a Roth could generate the necessary income to qualify for the write-off. Your CPA could back into this calculation to figure what the conversion amount needs to be.

Recession Conversion

Your account is down due to poor market conditions. This could also work for a particular stock or fund you think will realize significant growth in the next few years.

Because you pay income tax on the conversion amount it makes sense that significant losses may signal a time to convert. The smaller the value, the smaller the conversion tax. And if the market returns with a normal growth rate all your gains will be tax-free.

Social Security at one time was tax free. But now, depending on your income, up to 85% of your social security can be taxed. When converting to a Roth IRA you can easily exceed the threshold causing your benefits to be taxable when ordinarily they might not. Please see the Social Security chapter for the income thresholds.

Tax Credit Loss - As I stated earlier, one scenario that may favor a conversion would be the possibility of losing a favorable tax write-off as the result of no income. As you recall, this could be caused by NOL carryforwards.

Another side effect could be the opposite. A conversion could boost your income causing ineligibility for certain tax credits and deductions. For example, a family may become ineligible for the Hope of Lifetime Learning Credit if their income is too high the year they convert.

Medicare Part B Premiums, which pay mainly for doctor visits and outpatient services, are based on income levels. So, if your income is higher because of a conversion then you may pay higher premiums. In 2014, the standard premium stayed the same from 2013 at $104.90 a month. However, if your income exceeds $85,000 or more for single or $170,000 for a married couple who fie a joint tax return, then the premiums start to increase.

Why it might make sense to pay the higher Medicare Part B premium on a temporary basis is the requirement of distributions from a traditional IRA. Because traditional IRAs have RMDs you may have higher income for as long as you are forced to withdraw money.

Whereas if you converted to a Roth, which do not require RMDs, your income just may be low enough to escape higher premiums.

The unique method in which the Roth is taxed along with conversions and recharacterizations allow for some interesting strategies. A few can get complex but if you take the time it can save you a bundle.

A word you probably won't find in any dictionary. The IRS has a way with the English language. In this case recharacterization means 'undoing'. I also haven't figured out why the IRS added a half year to critical ages such as 59 ½ and 70 ½ either.

If you decide that converting to a Roth makes sense, it is always nice to know you can change your mind and eliminate the tax liability. The deadline for the recharacterizing is your tax filing deadline, including extensions. If you filed your tax or filed for an extension by the due date, you receive an automatic 6-month extension to complete your recharacterization. For calendar year filers, the 6-month extension expiries on October 15 2015 for recharacterizing a 2014 conversion.

If you need to recharacterize your conversion, contact your IRA custodian for information on the requirements and allow enough time for the paperwork to be processed. Recharacterizations must be earnings or losses. For help with this, contact your custodian, finance or tax pro, or use the formula provided by the IRS in Publication 590 available at http://www.irs.gov.

Conversions amounts that are recharacterized can be reconverted. The deadlines for these types of conversion are January 1, of the year in which the conversion occurred, or 30-days after the recharacterizations was completed if the reconversion occurs before this period, it is considered to be a failed conversion.

The amount also could be treated as a regular contribution to your Roth, which is subject to the limit of $5,500 for 2014 plus an additional $1,000 if you were at least age 50 by the end of the year. So if the conversion amount was above this limit or you already made your contribution to your Roth you now have an excess contribution. Are you having fun yet?

This excess amount, of course, must be removed from your Roth by your tax filing deadline including extensions. And don't forget that pesky NIA to properly clean up all traces of the failed conversion. The failure to remove the excess is a hefty penalty or everyone would over fund their Roth. It is 6% a year on the amount that shouldn't be there. Oh, and he amount is no longer eligible for tax free or tax deferred growth.

So please ensure this doesn't happen by double checking the eligibility of the conversion by contacting the custodian and by verifying the income reported on your tax return.

There is one more important aspect about recharacterization that must be mentioned. Earlier, I wrote that it rarely makes sense to pay the conversion tax using funds from the conversion.   Another supporting point for that view is if you decide to recharacterize , the funds taken from the IRA to pay the taxes can't be included as part of the recharacterization.

Because TIPRA allows everyone to convert to a Roth in 2010 but does not remove the income limitations fo contributing to a Roth I would imagine something new will begin happening. For those that a Roth makes sense yet have incomes that preclude them from creating one can try this strategy. Create a traditional IRA, fund it to their hearts content (within IRS limits) then convert it to a Roth the following year. Then simply wash, rinse, and repeat.

Probably the best way is to have two Roth's. One would receive your converted funds. If the account incurs losses within the first year then you can recharacterize so you don't have to pay income taxes on a value that no longer exists. If you don't recharacterize then simply transfer the assets to the other Roth. And repeat in subsequent years.

Some of the more sneaky readers may be wondering if they can convert assets to a Roth and if a particular investment does poorly they can 'cherry pick' the asset for recharacterization. I used the words 'cherry pick' purposely. In IRS Notice 2000-39, the IRS anticipated this and disseminated 'anti-cherry picking' rules. This rule stated Roth assets should prorate all gains and losses over the entire Roth instead of on an asset-by-asset basis.

But what can be done is separating uncorrelated investments or funds and converting each to its own Roth. For instance, separating Large Cap, Mid-cap, Small-Cap etc. and converting each to its own Roth. If any have poor performance then just recharacterize that particular investment or fund. Depending on the size of the conversion amount you may want to separate based on type of investment also. Examples would be separations based on consumer goods, energy, communications and transportation.

Normally, losses within an IRA aren't deductible. But you may be able to deduct a loss if you meet the following requirements:

1. You must be converting all your types of IRAs which include traditional IRAs, SEP IRAs, and Simple IRAs accounts.
2. All contributions must be nondeductible, or after-tax contributions
3. The total converted amount would have to be less than your basis or the value of your nondeductible contributions.

I briefly wrote about losses early in this appendix. Losses of various kinds can be used to offset Roth conversion income. As long as the loss is not considered to be passive it can be used to offset the income from a Roth conversion. The definition of a passive loss would be a loss incurred through a rental property, limited partnership, or other enterprise in which you are not actively involved.

Charitable contributions can also be carry-forwarded. For example, a contribution of $100,000 of stock to charity that you end up having to carry forward $50,000 of the deduction because your deduction exceeds the AGI threshold limitation. The $50,000 carryforward deduction can be applied against income from a Roth conversion.

If your income is $40,000 but you own a business and it suffers a loss of $50,000 for the year then you may become ineligible for any nonrefundable credits of any kind. However, if you convert to a Roth then the income reported may be just enough to make those credits available.

There are two reasons that converting to a Roth makes sense when estate taxes are an issue. If your estate will be paying estate taxes, Roth conversions usually always make sense. The first reason is based on how estates are taxed. Secondly, most traditional IRAs end up in trusts causing unforeseen issues.

In regards to how estates are taxed, traditional IRAs, qualified retirement plans and Roth IRAs are included in your estate upon your death. And, unlike most all other accounts, these accounts do not receive a step-up in basis when you pass away. Not the cost of the assets when purchased. Step-up in basis refers to the readjustment of appreciated assets to fair market value at inheritance. They do not receive this readjustment because they are deemed to be Income in Respect of a Decent (IRD). Think of IRD as an incompetent attempt by the IRS to fix the taxation of an estate.

The IRD is a deduction to help mitigate the effect of double-taxation. This double-taxation occurs because the IRS assesses an income tax on distributions that occur after the account owner's death.

And in some situations an estate tax has been imposed upon the same funds that are subject to income tax.

At first, it may appear that converting to a Roth for estate tax purposes doesn't make sense on an income tax perspective. The reason that it often does is because the IRD deduction is only allowed for federal estate taxes paid – not state estate taxes. So, if you convert while you are alive, you can take the full deduction, federal and state. If you wait until you pass away your estate will pay the taxes but your heirs will not get a corresponding state deduction.

The other estate planning issue and the less obvious one is based on the facts that most retirees have large IRAs that end up in trusts. Upon their deaths, the trusts become irrevocable. When your trust becomes irrevocable, it becomes an entity that must file tax returned subject to trust tax rates that are much higher relative to individual tax filer's rates. These problems can often be fixed by converting to a Roth.

This strategy involves the unfortunate circumstance of the eminent death of a spouse. This works because those that file single pay more income tax that those who file a joint income tax return. For example, a husband or wife are diagnosed with a medical condition and provided a shorter life expectancy than expected. Converting assets to a Roth IRA may make sense in this situation by paying taxes at the lower joint tax rates rather than waiting until the surviving spouse is in a higher single tax bracket. If you own highly appreciated company stock in your 401(k) or other company plan, this little-known tax break could be for you. It's called net unrealized appreciation (NUA) and can allow you to pull out all, or some, of your company stock when you rollover the rest of your assets into an IRA. (Company stock is defined as stock in the company that you work for). Before 2008, you had to roll your company plan into a traditional IRA and then roll it into a Roth. Now you can roll your company plan directly into a Roth IRA.

Here's how it works: You roll your company stock into a taxable account (non-IRA), and put the rest of you 401(k) assets into an IRA (traditional or Roth). You'd then pay tax on the stock based on the original cost. The difference – or the NUA – wouldn't be paid until you sell the shares. If the cost of the stock in your plan was $10, and now it's worth $50, your stock has appreciated by $40. This $40 is the NUA. The distribution can only qualify if there is a 'separation of service', reaching the age of 59 ½, death or disability.

The great thing about NUA is the taxation. It could be currently taxed at the low long-term capital gains rate, currently 15%. If you rolled it over into a traditional IRA with the rest of the assets and then withdrew those funds, it would be taxed as ordinary income, which could be double that of capital gains.

In 2008, a new law allowed conversions from 401(k)'s directly into Roths. Some thought a tax loophole was created and the NUA would never be taxed. Because you would pay tax on the cost basis (the original cost of the stock) upon conversion, just like you would, had you rolled your company stock separately into a taxable account.

But then upon withdraw of the stock from the Roth it would all be tax free, hence the NU Awa never taxed.

In IRS Notice 2009-75, the IRS has closed this loophole. They stated that a conversion from a company plan to a Roth is treated as if it was first converted to a traditional IRA then converted to a Roth. Meaning, the full conversion amount from the company plan will be taxed upon conversion to the Roth just as if it was converted to a traditional IRA. The NUA tax break is irrevocably lost. NUA can have an enormous impact on what's left to your heirs; but the parties involved must have a very clear understanding of the process. Taking advantage of NUA can affect the stepped-up value of the stock. The withdraw of company stock and rollover must be done in the same calendar year and the entire plan must be included in this technique, not just the company stock.

APPENDIX 2 – EXECUTIVE ORDER

By virtue of the authority vested in me by Section 5 (b) of the Act of October 6, 1917, as amended by Section 2 of the Act of March 9, 1933, entitled "An Act to provide relief in the existing national emergency in banking, and for other purposes," in which amendatory Act Congress declared that a serious emergency exists, I, Franklin D. Roosevelt, President of the United States of America, do declare that said national emergency still continues to exist and pursuant to said section do hereby prohibit the hoarding of gold coin, gold bullion, and gold certificates within the continental United States by individuals, partnerships, associations and corporations and hereby prescribe the following regulations for carrying out the purposes of this order:

Section 1. For the purposes of this regulation, the term "hoarding" means the withdrawal and withholding of gold coin, gold bullion or gold certificates from the recognized and customary channels of trade. The term "person" means any individual, partnership, association or corporation.

Section 2. All persons are hereby required to deliver on or before May 1, 1933, to a Federal Reserve Bank or a branch or agency thereof or to any member bank of the Federal Reserve System all gold coin, gold bullion and gold certificates now owned by them or coming into their ownership on or before April 28, 1933, except the following:

(a) Such amount of gold as may be required for legitimate and customary use in industry, profession or art within a reasonable time, including gold prior to refining and stocks of gold in reasonable amounts for the usual trade requirements of owners mining and refining such gold.

(b) Gold coin and gold certificates in an amount not exceeding in the aggregate $100 belonging to any one person; and gold coins having a recognized special value to collectors of rare and unusual coins.

(c) Gold coin and bullion earmarked or held in trust for a recognized foreign Government or foreign central bank or the Bank for International Settlements.

(d) Gold coin and bullion licensed for other proper transactions (not involving hoarding) including gold coin and bullion imported for reexport or held pending action on applications for export licenses.

Section 3. Until otherwise ordered any person becoming the owner of any gold coin, gold bullion, or gold certificates after April 28, 1933, shall, within three days after receipt thereof, deliver the same in the manner prescribed in Section 2; unless such gold coin, gold bullion or gold certificates are held for any of the purposes specified in paragraphs (a), (b), or (c) of Section 2; or unless such gold coin or gold bullion is held for purposes specified in paragraph (d) of Section 2 and the person holding it is, with respect to such gold coin or bullion, a licensee or applicant for license pending action thereon.

Section 4. Upon receipt of gold coin, gold bullion or gold certificates delivered to it in accordance with Sections 2 or 3, the Federal Reserve Bank or member bank will pay therefor an equivalent amount of any other form of coin or currency coined or issued under the laws of the United States.

Section 5. Member banks shall deliver all gold coin, gold bullion and gold certificates owned or received by them (other than as exempted under the provisions of Section 2) to the Federal Reserve

Banks of their respective districts and receive credit or payment therefor.

Section 6. The Secretary of the Treasury, out of the sum made available to the President by Section 501 of the Act of March 9, 1933, will in all proper cases pay the reasonable costs of transportation of gold coin, gold bullion or gold certificates delivered to a member bank or Federal Reserve Bank in accordance with Section 2, 3, or 5 hereof, including the cost of insurance, protection, and such other incidental costs as may be necessary, upon production of satisfactory evidence of such costs. Voucher forms for this purpose may be procured from Federal Reserve Banks.

Section 7. In cases where the delivery of gold coin, gold bullion or gold certificates by the owners thereof within the time set forth above will involve extraordinary hardship or difficulty, the Secretary of the Treasury may, in his discretion, extend the time within which such delivery must be made. Applications for such extensions must be made in writing under oath, addressed to the Secretary of the Treasury and filed with a Federal Reserve Bank. Each application must state the date to which the extension is desired, the amount and location of the gold coin, gold bullion and gold certificates in respect of which such application is made and the facts showing extension to be necessary to avoid extraordinary hardship or difficulty.

Section 8. The Secretary of the Treasury is hereby authorized and empowered to issue such further regulations as he may deem necessary to carry out the purposes of this order and to issue licenses thereunder, through such officers or agencies as he may designate, including licenses permitting the Federal Reserve Banks and member banks of the Federal Reserve System, in return for an equivalent amount of other coin, currency or credit, to deliver, earmark or hold in trust gold coin and bullion to or for persons showing the need for the same for any of the purposes specified in paragraphs (a), (c) and (d) of Section 2 of these regulations.

Section 9. Whoever willfully violates any provision of this Executive Order or of these regulations or of any rule, regulation or license issued thereunder may be fined not more than $10,000, or, if a natural person, may be imprisoned for not more than ten years, or both; and any officer, director, or agent of any corporation who knowingly participates in any such violation may be punished by a like fine, imprisonment, or both.

This order and these regulations may be modified or revoked at any time.

POSTMASTER: PLEASE POST IN A CONSPICUOUS PLACE.—JAMES A. FARLEY, Postmaster General

UNDER EXECUTIVE ORDER OF THE PRESIDENT

Issued April 5, 1933

all persons are required to deliver

ON OR BEFORE MAY 1, 1933

all GOLD COIN, GOLD BULLION, AND GOLD CERTIFICATES now owned by them to a Federal Reserve Bank, branch or agency, or to any member bank of the Federal Reserve System.

Executive Order

[Two columns of small-print legal text of the Executive Order forbidding the hoarding of gold coin, gold bullion and gold certificates, signed FRANKLIN D. ROOSEVELT, The White House, April 5, 1933.]

For Further Information Consult Your Local Bank

GOLD CERTIFICATES may be identified by the words "GOLD CERTIFICATE" appearing thereon. The serial number and the Treasury seal on the face of a GOLD CERTIFICATE are printed in YELLOW. Be careful not to confuse GOLD CERTIFICATES with other issues which are redeemable in gold but which are not GOLD CERTIFICATES. Federal Reserve Notes and United States Notes are "redeemable in gold" but are not "GOLD CERTIFICATES" and are not required to be surrendered

Special attention is directed to the exceptions allowed under Section 2 of the Executive Order

CRIMINAL PENALTIES FOR VIOLATION OF EXECUTIVE ORDER
$10,000 fine or 10 years imprisonment, or both, as provided in Section 9 of the order

Secretary of the Treasury.

U.S. Government Printing Office: 1933 2-16064

APPENDIX 3 – REIT REQUIREMENTS

Below are the requirements for the types of REITs discussed in this book.

- Kansas residents only: In addition to the suitability requirements described above, it is recommended that investors should invest no more than 10% of their liquid net worth in non-traded REITS shares and securities of other real estate investment trusts. "Liquid net worth" is defined as that portion of net worth (total assets minus total liabilities) that is comprised of cash, cash equivalents and readily marketable securities.

- Alabama residents only: In addition to the suitability standards above, shares will only be sold to Alabama residents that represent that they have a liquid net worth of at least 10 times the amount of their investment in non-traded REITS and other similar programs.

- Nebraska residents only: Investors must have either (a) a net worth of $350,000 or (b) a net worth of $100,000 and an annual income of $70,000. The investor's maximum investment in non-traded REITS should not exceed 10% of the investor's net worth

- Kentucky residents only: Investors must have either (a) a net worth of $250,000 or (b) a gross annual income of at least $70,000 and a net worth of at least $70,000, with the amount invested in NON-TRADED REITS offerings not to exceed 10% of the Kentucky investor's liquid net worth.

- Massachusetts, Ohio, Oregon and New Mexico residents only: Investors must have either (a) a minimum net worth of at least $250,000 or (b) an annual gross income of at least $70,000 and a net worth of at least $70,000. The investor's maximum investment in non-traded REITS cannot exceed 10% of the Oregon or New Mexico resident's net worth. It shall be unsuitable for a Massachusetts or Ohio investor's aggregate investment in shares of non-traded real estate investment trusts to exceed ten percent (10%) of his, her or its liquid net worth. "Liquid net worth" shall be defined as that portion of net worth (total assets exclusive of primary residence, home furnishings and automobiles minus liabilities) that is comprised of cash, cash equivalents and readily marketable securities.

- Pennsylvania and Michigan residents only: A Pennsylvania or Michigan investor cannot invest more than 10% of their net worth in non-traded REITS.

- Iowa residents only: The maximum investment allowable in non-traded REITS is 10% of an Iowa investor's liquid net worth. Liquid net worth is defined as that portion of net worth (total assets minus total liabilities) that is comprised of cash, cash equivalents and readily marketable securities.

- New Jersey residents only: A New Jersey investor must have either (a) a minimum liquid net worth of $100,000 and an annual income of $85,000 or (b) a minimum liquid net worth of $350,000. In addition, a New Jersey investor's total investment in non-traded REITS shall not exceed 10% of his or her liquid net worth. "Liquid net worth" is defined as that portion of net worth (total assets exclusive of home, home furnishings and automobiles, minus total liabilities) that is comprised of cash, cash equivalents and readily marketable securities.

- Tennessee residents only: A Tennessee resident's maximum investment in non-traded REITS shares shall not exceed 10% of his or her liquid net worth (exclusive of home, home furnishings and automobiles).

- Missouri residents only: In addition to the suitability requirements described above, no more than ten percent (10%) of any one (1) Missouri investor's liquid net worth shall be invested in non-traded REITS securities registered with the Securities Division.

- California residents only: In addition to the general suitability requirements described above, California investors' maximum investment in non-traded REITS shares shall not exceed 10% of the investor's net worth (exclusive of home, home furnishings and automobile).

- North Dakota residents only: North Dakota investors must represent that, in addition to the general suitability standards listed above, they have a net worth of at least ten times their investment in the non-traded REITS.

Dan Casey

Dan Casey